HINDSIGHT

VOLUME 2

DUSTIN K. JESSIP

author·HOUSE·

AuthorHouse™
1663 Liberty Drive
Bloomington, IN 47403
www.authorhouse.com
Phone: 1 (800) 839-8640

Published by AuthorHouse 06/19/2020

ISBN: 978-1-7283-6257-1 (sc)
ISBN: 978-1-7283-6256-4 (e)

Special Thanks

There have been a few people involved with this project that I would like to thank in the sincerest way a book can.

Cheyenne, you took time out of your already crazy schedule to help me with my dream. You did some much needed editing, which has helped me tremendously. I sincerely appreciate your time, dedication, and inspiration. I am so grateful to have you in my life.

Battle, you know who you are. Your advice, insight and support have contributed so much to the writing I do and the author I want to become. I appreciate you and I am glad you are who you are.

To everyone that believed in Hindsight Volume 1 by either purchasing a copy or providing feedback that I look forward to, I appreciate every one of you. It is my hope that you continue finding value in my words as you kindly donate your time to what I have to share with you. Thank you all!

CONTENTS

INTRODUCTION

Building on the words in Hindsight Volume 1, Volume 2 is designed to help integrate a rejuvenated Perspective with a more in-depth logic and continued theory. You are invited to add to what you already know as we continue to navigate socially Acceptable ideas that often brush up against twisted humor. More seriously, this is a way for you to continue asking questions that will ultimately inhibit your own critical thinking skills. The overall goal of the Hindsight Volumes is to get your mind to switch gears with ease as you learn to Accept people for who they are and *how* they are.

It is going to be critical for society to grow *together*, not as individuals or groups interacting with other individuals or groups. We are one people, breathing the same air, treading the same waters, all on our own journeys through life. Mutual Respect is a must, especially as technology progresses, communication broadens and ideas can flourish, or collide with other ideas.

I will keep this short and sweet, as many of you that absorbed Volume 1 should have a decent idea of what to expect. This volume is a little more Focused and certainly deeper than the last. I would also like to provide a similar disclaimer here, as I did in Volume 1, I am in no way racist, sexist, extremist or biased in any other ways than I will openly admit. Any stereotypical comparisons are simply used as a point of reference, not necessarily shared belief. My sole intention is to help open minds and contribute to an improved society for everyone to live in happily.

With that being said, please do not take offense to anything I say. Instead, I ask that you take the words as they come for what they are: words. They are there for you to do with them what you will. They are they to inspire free-thought and Creativity. They are there to convict those that accept and desire inspiration. They are there to help *me* form my own Perspective as I continue to learn and grow in this world because I too need to continue doing so. The day we stop learning is the day we cease to live a meaningful life, in my complete and honest opinion. Obviously, circumstances dictate some scenarios in this Context, but for the most part, I believe it makes sense.

In any case, I encourage you to read Volume 1 before you read Volume 2. It may seem like it should not matter, but I assure you, it does. The foundation laid out in Volume 1 Creates a base understanding for Perception building aligned with Respect. The small but critical lessons throughout Volume 1 are evident throughout Volume 2, some more obvious than others. As you absorb the words before you, I also encourage you to make them your own. How they relate to you in your life both past and present. More effectively, how will you let them resonate within your thoughts moving forward? These are the few things I ask you to Consider as you move on into what I think is an important journey. Again, I thank you for your time and I sincerely hope you enjoy Hindsight Volume 2.

CHAPTER 1

PIECES OF PEACE

SERENITY

se-ren-i-ty

NOUN

1. the state of being calm, peaceful and untroubled.

"Surround yourself with a peaceful
environment to help achieve **Serenity**."

In a time of overwhelming information availability, we expose ourselves to so many stressors every single day. Whether we choose the media we take in, or it finds its way into our subconscious through other means by way of background noise & visuals, it is impossible to ignore every bit of what we may not want. Unless you walk around with noise-cancelling headphones and blinders and can still somehow manage to Focus *only* on what you are trying to, chances are you're going to get blindsided by someone partaking in life like a semi-normal human being, carrying their venti vanilla latte while they're nodding to Maroon 5 in their ear buds. Hopefully they're coordinated enough to save the coffee from staining your highwaters or converses when they're too oblivious to notice you noticing them not notice you.

Don't get too worked up, this is not a fashion judgement, but a way to say hey, no one is impervious to information exposure unless you are both deaf and blind OR you are completely off the grid and unplugged from the technical world. According to an article on Lifehack.org, "Researchers indicate that technology and the noise of urban areas constantly demand our attention and disturb us from Focusing, which taxes our cognitive functions." (Rogers, 2019, para.5)

Urban areas have slowly but surely taken over quite a bit of real estate in the last century, which is concurrent with the growth of technology. Coincidence? Absolutely not. Technology has sped up so many things, such as communication, transportation, medicine production in workplaces, etc. As technology expands, it inhibits growth in each of the aforementioned sectors of the market. As each of those markets grow, so do jobs, companies, supply and demand for the associated goods(hypothetically) and the *information* made available for it.

This is an important time to reflect on the chapter about Focus in Volume 1. Remember, information is free, and there is A LOT of *free* information. It is up to you to first decide what information is actually relevant to you, then more importantly to decipher the information for what it's really trying to achieve. Nothing can be more misleading than the word FREE. This may very well be a contradictory position for some of you, which is great. Either way, think about it, thoroughly.

The information bombarding us at any given time while we walk through a supermarket or scroll through social media on our mobile devices will ever increasingly be fine-tuned to fit *us*, based on past search history, purchases and even places visited or checked-in to. That data is collected, analyzed and used to target you, very specifically with a marketing scheme behind it.

Now, this is not a re-hash about Focus. This is merely an illustration of what a typical individual may encounter on a daily basis. From the morning routine coffee, checking emails or work orders, to attending meetings or picking up on a project from the day before, to taking your lunch at your favorite spot every Wednesday, or finally buttoning up projects or work hours fulfilled so you can finally go home, everyone has *some* kind of routine. Our routines are routines. Engrained in our brains, allowing us to go on autopilot, which subsequently allows our subconscious to wonder. This exposes our direct attention to a bunch of different streams of information, subjecting our stress levels to heights that have been normalized. Whether we are on autopilot or not, the information streaming by us at any given time is unmeasurable to say the least.

If you can relate to even a shred of this, ask yourself: Are you ready for a vacation? Undoubtedly, the majority of the answers are going to be a hard "YES", followed by a "Why is that even a question?". Why is vacation something we all long for (for the most part)? Vacations are an oasis we imagine freeing our minds from the constant strain we face every week. Kids, school, extra-curriculars, work, deadlines, projects, friends, families, hobbies, bills, etc., all take a toll on our mental capacity and we need to find time to unplug.

In fact, this is a great time to go read the article cited above. The link is available in the References portion at the end of this book. Take the few minutes it will take you to absorb its message, then Consider how it applies to you and where you could go to take a hike or at least get away from a suburban area. We all owe it to ourselves to give our brains a break, and frankly, it is essential to our mental health.

Unplug and limit technical and informational exposure. Give your brain a chance to unwind as it absorbs nature. You know, trees, grass, and smog-free blue sky. Find your backdrop. If you're near the ocean, get closer to it, and further away from the cityscape. If you're near mountains, go mountain. If you're from the Midwest…go sit in a cornfield? Ha. Just kidding, unless you're into that. Beware of combines, by the way. Seriously, there are state parks well within driving range for many of you. Take advantage of them. Do yourself, co-workers, family, friends and therapists/bartenders a favor. Find your backdrop, find Serenity.

Now, this is going to be a temporary getaway (most likely). That's okay, as long as we can make a commitment to find our Serenity on a more consistent schedule, then that's all we can do. Life will go on either way, but how well we let ourselves decompress so we can allow ourselves achieve better problem-solving, Creativity and overall mental health will ultimately dictate how effective we are as we move forward. In a way, we cannot afford not to give ourselves a break, as life will catch up to us eventually anyway.

The Takeaway: Finding peace is imperative to maintaining sanity. This seems obvious enough, yet many of us are gluttons for punishment and allow ourselves to get pushed to the limit before we finally snap and push back. We need to do our best to avoid snapping. We need to find a backdrop and go there consistently to achieve Serenity for the sake of our mental health as well as humanity.

For those wondering if they were going to see the famous quote or not, here it is:

"Grant me the Serenity to Accept the things I cannot change, the courage to change the things I can and the Wisdom to know the difference." -Reinhold Niebuhr

CHAPTER 2

THE GIFT THAT KEEPS ON GIVING

GENEROSITY

gen-er-os-i-ty

NOUN

1. the quality of being king and generous.

> "A simple act of **Generosity** lead to several more
> acts of kindness, therefore reversing the negative
> aura that had once tainted the mood."

Your very act of reading these words is an act of Generosity. You may not believe so or question how. The time you are spending behind these words suggest a few things about who you are: 1. You are interested in what I have to say, so *I* appreciate you and your time. 2. You are interested in helping yourself, which is a great example for others to follow. 3. You are a kind and generous soul anyway and you support those that seek ways to be Generous as well. 4. Helping yourself or not, you are likely to help others and probably have before, which is exactly what we are going to be looking at.

No matter where you fall on the spectrum of Generosity, one small act can have an everlasting impact. Real quick, can you remember a time when you have been a part of or witnessed a Random Act of Kindness (RAK)?

For no reason at all, other than to simply do a good deed, someone bought a stranger's meal, coffee or fuel at a gas station. Why? What domino effect just came into those lives involved, no matter which role *you* played in that *one* act of Generosity.

Since we are unable to gather every individual story (not necessarily a random act, mind you), I'm left to tell you *one* of mine, for now. It was a blustery day in Johnston, Iowa. Many National Guard Soldiers had travelled far and wide to attend drill at Camp Dodge. There is a gas station not far from the Main Gate, where thousands of Soldiers stop in every year. On one particular morning, I was filling up my gas tank and grabbing a coffee for myself and a few others. When I went to pay, the cashier gave me an abnormally low amount. With a quizzical look, I told him I also needed to pay for my fuel, which was well over $50. He kindly informed me that a man had paid for it already. In fact, he paid for the fuel of over a half dozen other Soldiers that morning as well. If memory serves me correctly, I believe he reportedly worked for a car dealership in the area.

Like the other Soldiers, I was grateful as I was Motivated to pay it forward. Say what you will about the National Guard or the Army, but typically, we worked long days, especially when we were not in our Home Station. Camp Dodge was not my Home Station, so a long day was inevitable. A long day that you know is coming can often be daunting, especially to those untrained or unprepared to take one on.

That one act of Generosity set the tone for the rest of the (long) day. It's always hard to imagine what would not have happened in our past until it is long gone, and we can put what we know now (when we look back) into Perspective. That one simple, long day could very well have been another day in the Army for all of us, but it was a day that sticks out, and for good reason. I cannot speak for the other recipients that morning, as we were not training directly together. What I can tell you is that $50+ went towards the lunch for myself and a few other Soldiers, as well as a 20% tip for the server waiting on us that day. And where do you suppose the continued Generosity went then? Who knows? In all honesty, it really does not matter. That's the beauty of Generosity.

If it is your sole intention to be nice to someone to only gain a favor, to indebt them to you for your "kindness", then you are not being kind at all. In fact, you are setting yourself and the other party up for failure. Without the conscious Acceptance that your act of kindness/Generosity may never be repaid, then it was never Generosity to begin with. Understand and Accept that now if you have not already.

This is also a good time to reflect on moments in your life when you may have shown Generosity to another. How did they react? How did it affect life thereafter? What was your *true* intention/what did you want out of it? The broadest answer should be nothing at all, but alas, we are human. Surely you would appreciate reciprocation to some degree, whether it be returned to you or at least dedicated to you in some fashion down the road.

This is a concept that takes a great deal of Selflessness, Patience and Integrity. Your true intent should be to inspire your recipients to pay it forward. It requires Patience because the effects of your acts may take a very long time to come to fruition, if you ever see it at all. And Integrity is a key player because if your intent is truly Selfless, then you will be able to complete your act of Generosity and never openly seek thanks or recognition of any kind. This is probably the hardest part of being Generous. As humans, we seek to feel loved, Accepted and appreciated, especially when we do good. That moment of adoration is completely desirable, but selfish. There is a bigger picture that we all have to paint together. It will require generations to make happen, but it is more than worth it.

Meet despair with sympathy and solution where applicable. Meet anger with tolerance and calm. Greet your neighbor with wholesome intent. Always be kind and when you are able, be Generous, truly Generous. No limelight, no thank you. Remember that you may very well be the recipient of true Generosity if you have not been already. The ripples of Generosity should always be encouraged to continue throughout eternity. Should every like-minded individual adopt this concept and do their absolute best to contribute to the cause, then the world is sure to become a happier place.

Do this, and you can thank yourself. You can be the difference and you can continue making ripples, keep the domino effect going. Be a part of the bigger picture and help shape a more meaningful society. The more of us that contribute, the more likely we are to see results sooner. This is a way of life that should become normal, not random. If you're at least Considering what you can do to make the difference, thank you. This might be the only one you get.

The Takeaway: You do not have to spend hundreds of dollars or pay for someone's coffee without them knowing. You can simply start by holding the door open for someone. Tell your co-worker when they have a booger hanging out of their nose, or just laugh at a stupid joke after you imagine your co-worker with a booger hanging from their nose. In all seriousness, Generosity takes a lot of character. All I can really ask at this point is that you deliver an act of Generosity where you are comfortable, but never expect one when you're not.

CHAPTER 3

TRIPLE SEVENS

LUCK

luck

NOUN

1. success or failure apparently brought by chance rather than through one's own actions.

"The fact that he won a jackpot on his first spin was pure **Luck**."

A diverse term often associated with things like rabbits' feet, elephants, horseshoes, keys, four leaf clovers, or any other sentimental objects held in regard as lucky, is usually called a Lucky charm. If someone steps in a pile of horse manure without knowing, they might be pretty upset to soil their loafers. Should they be grateful they just completed a superstitious act that brings Luck? Would you believe it's Lucky to break bottles of alcohol on accident in Japan, is this really a thing? According to Raga (2016), "…a clumsy bartender in Okinawa, Japan felt humiliated and assumed he would be in big trouble. Instead, the owner and patrons cheered because they believed that breaking the bottle brings good luck and higher profits to the bar. Intentionally knocking alcohol bottles onto the floor isn't auspicious though-it has to be an accident." (para.14)

This bartender may not have been so cheerfully Accepted if he was working for the guy with road apples on his fancy shoes, as the custom in (American) business is more along the lines of "You break it, you buy it".

But as Luck would have it, the bartender in Okinawa is safe for now, maybe sent by Mr. Loafers to sabotage Mr. Okinawa's Bar because he neglected a business transaction involving illegally smuggled elephants, which Mr. Okinawa counter-sabotaged by making Mr. Loafers step in his own horse's piles of what Mr. Okinawa thought of the deal to begin with. *Phew.*

What's up with a dangling foot being "Lucky"? Now I need to know, for real. You don't need to Google it; I'm literally doing it for us. Lucky you. According to Dove (2015), "The belief that a rabbit's foot could be charmed, and therefore help one lead a charmed life, began as an offshoot of totemism. This belief in a spiritual connection between humans and other living beings dates back thousands of years." (para.3)

There. Partially satisfied? No? Me either. I guess the rabbits were believed to have a greater connection to powerful forces because they lived underground and were therefore closer to them, so their feet, in particular, could be harvested and then carried around for good Luck.

Moving on. Luck is merely a subject of Perception, or Deception. Depending on each situation and the circumstances associated with each, Luck may be good, bad or completely irrelevant. A favorite misconception of Luck I witness frequently is when an employee is clocking out for the day just as another is clocking in for theirs. The fresh employee might say something along the lines of; "Oh, you're leaving for the day? Lucky you." Man, do you realize what you just said? The employee leaving did their time. You work overnights and clock out at 8:30am and then listen to someone tell you how Lucky you are. Have you ever worked overnights? No? Great idea. I have, and I'll tell you right now, overnight shifts are not *Lucky* to be going home after their shift is up. They/we worked for it, all damn night. Thanks, have a great day. Lucky day shifter.

Speaking of day shift, who here has a favorite team from any sport that is televised on national television? Good, then you might be able to relate. Does your team win or lose when you do/don't watch them? Do you have to wear a certain article of clothing to hinder how they perform? What about going to the fridge to replenish your purple mountains, squeeze a lime and call Tony or reminisce the bud knight? At the end of the day, find someone else who has similar superstitions and start documenting. Post your results for the world to see and compare so you can realize how much it really doesn't matter. (Smiley face) Though I would be super intrigued if someone out there was Lucky enough to actually have something real. Please prove me wrong!

So, people win the lottery, or jackpots or free trips to the hospital if they quit breathing in a public place (I'm not sure how true that is, so please don't take my word for it and just chuckle like I was hoping for. Thanks!) There are absolutely winners out there, but there is a little word associated to bettors all around the world that makes all the difference; Odds. You see, the difference between the average gambler and a bettor is typically how familiar one is with what they're betting on, as well as how they go about it.

Anyone of legal betting age can pick a bunch of random numbers and pray for a winning lottery ticket, or for their Keno machine to turn their $2.00 bet into $1500.00. Random picks will deliver random paybacks, including none at all. The disciplines of probability and statistics are often used by more polished bettors than the average gambler. Their more calculated picks are applied to sports betting, horse racing, poker, of course keno and virtually any other games the house uses to make money off people eager to make "big money". While bettors are not always successful, their *odds* are Considerably more likely to be more accurate than those that do not make calculations at all, unless they're *Lucky*.

Again, this can be a matter of Perception as much as it can be Deception. Say a regular, established gambler is playing $5.00 a hand at video poker. He never seems to run out of money and keeps to himself. After an hour of gambling and on his last bet, he hits a taxable jackpot for $2,000.00. Unenthused, the man winced when employees and patrons nearby congratulate him on his "winnings". A patron sitting just outside earshot of the jackpot winner makes a remark about him being "Lucky". The man collects his cash and leaves for the day. Employees go about their business and patrons that were close by, continue discussing the jackpot, wishing they could get that "Lucky".

What a lot of people do not know or could simply not be aware of is that the man that won the jackpot had spent $500.00 a day for the last four days, trying to get a winning hand he had finally hit that day. He had spent $2,000.00 already that week, then paid taxes on the money he basically got back. All-in-all, he just paid taxes on money he had already paid taxes on. Not so "Lucky". Now, this is not every poker player or scenario, but it is also not entirely inaccurate. Poker players know that when they gamble, they have greater control over the *odds* in video poker than any other machine in the casino, which is why they keep coming back, longing to finally hit the Royal Flush for the maximum payout. I looked the odds up for us, but I am not willing to cite another source so when I say it's hard as hell to get a Royal Flush, believe me. If you don't, ask Mr. Loafers after he cleans his shoes off with your bathrobe. You don't have a bathrobe? Weird.

As you may have seen, Luck is a matter of where you are in the room when it strikes, if it really did at all. In all honesty, Luck is often taken for granted because of a rudimentary association of the word. It's easy to say three 7's in a row is Lucky, or that walking away from hitting a tree at 60mph in your car is Lucky (maybe that one really was), but is it Acceptable to feel Lucky to just be alive right now? Again, it depends on your Perception. If you have experienced a near-death experience, I'm sure you can agree to an extent that you are *Lucky* to be alive. Soldiers returning from a two-week field exercise may Consider themselves Lucky to take a shower. Better yet, someone that witnessed another person make a mistake may feel Lucky it was not them, and they'll take the experience and apply it to life as they move forward.

Luck is Luck, to an extent. Crazy things happen, but the odds were always there anyway, we just don't always see them because there is so much going on all the time. This is just easier and socially Acceptable to chalk it up to Luck. Now, depending on the socially Acceptable norm(s), the likeliness that Luck is repeated and prosperous is dictated by how society & circumstances react to whatever is Considered Lucky. The bar in Okinawa may very well experience greater sales after the bartender broke a bottle on accident, because they *believe* in the superstition and react accordingly.

Mr. Loafers on the other hand, may watch his horse win a couple more races, but he ends up in a bowling bag before all is said and done. Chalk it up to Luck wherever you want, but no one liked him anyway. (Kudos to those of you that know what I'm referencing.)

Ah! The name of the chapter. How many of you visualized a slot machine with big red 7's? Well, what if I named the chapter specifically for the United States Army Artillery? The M777 is a lightweight howitzer that delivers great accuracy on the battlefield. A common nickname for this beast; Triple Seven. Lucky for us, not so Lucky for whomever is on the other side.

The Takeaway: It is okay to have superstitions and good Luck charms or rituals. It's also okay to believe that every time you make a certain gesture or wear your Lucky T-shirt that your team is destined to win. However, don't get upset when it doesn't work. Take Luck for what it is; a matter of Perception. The lower your expectations are, the Luckier you will be, unless you're downrange of a Triple 7, then you're kind of screwed. Good Luck with that!

BOOMERANG

LOYALTY & TRUST

loy-al-ty & trust

NOUN

1. a strong feeling of support or allegiance.

> "When you earn Respect and gain Trust,
> then **Loyalty** should be returned."

NOUN

1. firm belief in the Reliability, truth, ability, or strength of someone or something.

> "Someone you let go must value your **Trust**
> in them to come back to you."

A term often associated with partner expectations or dogs; Loyalty is a trait that may very well be the epitome of any relationship's long-term success. Without a mutual sense of Trust, Respect or Confidence that your counterpart will return without question, Loyalty is doomed to fail or not exist at all.

These are things we sometimes fail to realize we have with someone else until they are either tested or broken altogether. They go hand-in-hand

and must be Respected accordingly. This does not mean that one who is Trustworthy is also Loyal and vice versa. Loyalty *should* indicate a strong sense of Trust, but it is not always so. Loyalty can take on a wide range of applications, such as where we purchase our groceries to whom we decide to lay next to on any given night.

We may have a degree of allegiance to any number of places, people, things or even ideas. However, that does not insinuate our undying Trust is tied to any of it. And the same is true going the other way; the said places, people, things or ideas may not have any Trust or Loyalty to *you.*

Okay, I'm boring myself. Maybe I am subliminally struggling to put thoughts to paper because these are difficult topics to paint about. Everyone wants to feel Trust and Loyalty to some degree. We test this more often than we consciously recognize, but the reality is, Trust and Loyalty are returned from those we have mutual Respect with and can be completely honest with.

Think of your deepest, darkest secret. If more than three other living people know about this secret, then dig deeper. If you cannot think of a deep dark secret, then think of something that only you and one other person on the face of this earth know about. Got it? Great. Now imagine logging onto social media and posting exactly what you thought of to share with everyone.

What would happen? How would the one other person feel about you and what you did? That is what we call betrayal. An act that destroys Trust. Intentional or not, Confidence was instilled in your competence to protect knowledge of a delicate matter. It doesn't stop there; by betraying someone that Trusted you with knowledge that only the two of you shared, you also show the individual you shared it with that you cannot be Trusted, unless that was your intention from the beginning. If that is the case, then you are an agent of Deception.

This is quite common for members of our law enforcement departments and agencies. The scale of which Deception is applied may vary depending on the mission at hand. Organized crime, biker gangs and stores selling CBD illegally (eyeroll) have all been brought down by undercover agents at some point or many points throughout history. The agent did not simply walk into the life and instantly gain Respect or Trust, they had to earn it.

Much like any new relationship, they start small. A greeting, an intervention during a bar fight or simply walking into a store trying get the store owner to sell them something to help them relieve pain. The initial contact opens the door for the agent to learn about the person they interact with. These people that are targeted are most likely found to be the weak link in an organization. Maybe they are at the bottom of the totem pole. Maybe they are a second in command, but not treated the way they feel they should be, or maybe they are the only link and therefore the subject of the described Deception.

For someone that understands the Intelligence process, let me provide some insight here; the agent is most likely a subject matter expert on their target already. They should already have days to weeks of behavioral patterns, schedules, eating habits, spending patterns and common locations their subject is most likely to travel to, depending on circumstances. We are all creatures of habit and if someone started watching you without you knowing, how hard to you think it would be for them to dissect your life in a matter of two weeks or less? Please don't get paranoid and start looking out your window for people that are not actually following you around, you're probably not as interesting as the people the law enforcement agents are going after. (No offense intended.)

Moving on. The agent that probably has a pretty good idea about their target is highly likely to build Trust rather quickly. The agent will demonstrate a level of Respect the target is either in need of or actively looking for. The "weak link", as it were, is vulnerable. We all get vulnerable. It is at these very moments we pretend we are heavily guarded, but we still open up to someone at some point, setting them up for an unparalleled amount of Trust for the rest of each your lives, or failure destined to bring the relationship to an end when that Trust is not reciprocated.

The agent, in this case, starts with Respect. The mutual Respect is paramount to gaining honesty, which leads to building the foundation of Trust. A simple interaction leads to a deeper conversation, revolving around what the agent *knows* the target will be intrigued by. The conversation leads to more interactions, more opportunities to show Respect and gain Trust.

Let's take a timeout for just a second. I want to throw a name out there that you should be aware of, so you do not apply everything we are talking about to your own life. This is an example specifically related to law enforcement. It is an example I am using to demonstrate how earning Respect to gain Trust and eventually Loyalty, in a very Deceptive manner, in order to bring criminals to justice. If you are not a part of criminal activity, then you have a lot less to worry about. The name; Donnie Brasco. It is a film based on an FBI agent working to target a crime family in New York. I will not go any further into detail, but if you have no idea what I am talking about and are into these topics, I highly advise you to take the time to research the story or at least watch the film.

Anyway, if the agent is successful, they spend weeks, months or even years getting to their ultimate goal, which is typically gathering enough incriminating evidence to put criminals behind bars for a very long time. That's it. They spend a lot of their time being someone they are not, to achieve an underlying agenda in the name of justice.

The point here is, be careful with who you Trust. Be careful with whom you align Loyalty, because unless that Trust and Loyalty are truly reciprocated, your relationship is doomed anyway. Beware of Deception and the possibility of alternate motives. The same goes for you, be aware of what you hope to achieve by gaining someone's Respect, Trust and Loyalty. It is very much a two-way street that you both need to be aware of. If you are two cars passing in the night, let it be that and nothing more. If you are heading in the same direction, make sure you want to end up at the same destination, so you know how long you'll be travelling in the same direction for.

The Takeaway: In case you did not hear me before; When you earn Respect, you gain Trust. When you gain Trust, you can begin to build Loyalty. It takes a monumental amount of time to build a reputation, and your Trustworthiness and Loyalties should be apparent in that reputation. Be aware of your true intentions, for that reputation that takes so long to build can be completely destroyed in a matter of seconds.

CHAPTER 5

MORE HUMAN THAN HUMAN

SELFLESSNESS

self-less-ness

NOUN

1. concern more with the needs and wishes of others than one's own.

"Sacrificing something we love in order to demonstrate dedication to another requires a great deal of **Selflessness**."

In a world where people stand in lines, sit in traffic or otherwise, impatiently waiting their turns to do whatever it is *they* need to do, one variable that each person has on their minds, subconsciously or otherwise; How much longer do *they* have to wait? What is taking so long? What do *I* need to do next?

Our Focus is very much on ourselves, as it really should and makes sense to be. We tend to handle what is on our plate as best we can. We do what we need to do and go on our way. There are interactions with others, doing the exact same thing. They are stocking shelves, loading trucks, serving food, checking charts, writing speeding tickets, playing sports, reading this book (probably not, but it's fun to imagine), or just out having a good time with friends & family.

So, we go out into the world dressed as best we could for what we had planned for the day. We bump into our co-workers, acquaintances, clients, patients, subjects, friends, family, and everyone else that comes within six feet of us throughout all the activities we are a part of. All the while, we exchange information; what we did the night before, asking about weather, asking how a project is going, asking if pain has subsided, asking why you were going twelve mph over the speed limit, etc.

All these conversations and questions are great in their respective places with the right type of person we are asking. However, at the end of the day, do they really matter? What does either person have to gain from what they have said to one another? This is the question I urge you to ask yourself both before and after you interact with someone. If you talk to a lot of people throughout the day, then I encourage you to start small. Pick the first person you talk to that you have never thought of outside of your limited transactions before.

What do we really hope to achieve when we engage in small talk? Filling the void of silence until your transaction is complete? Most likely. I am not saying we should try to be friends with every person ever, but I do want to explore the possibilities of getting into a real meaningful conversation with a complete stranger, or actually getting past the greetings and regular business transaction "conversations".

For all the Hospitality folks out there, this is *your* ground. Greeting patrons or clients, making them feel welcome and as special as we can while ultimately keeping them coming back to our workplaces are the things that are expected of us. The difference between meeting the standard expectation and *exceeding* the expectation is making each transaction unique to the person/people *you* are dealing with. Anyone can wait on a table, asking what someone wants to drink and eat, then deliver exactly what they asked for. Failing to make conversation or deliver in between interactions, is as copy-paste as the industry can get, and it belongs in a drive-thru where interaction is not much of an expectation to begin with. Give me my cheeseburger so I can mow down and get moving again. (Thank you!)

Hospitality or not, we are all humans, destined to interact with another human at some point. Why not make the most of it? Before you think to yourself something along the lines; "Nobody has time for that." Or

"There's no point.", then you're really in need of looking deeper at life and how you affect it.

I've said it before, and I'll say it again; your words have weight, meaning. No matter how limited a transaction is or may seem, it still holds value. The less human we are with one another, the less we instill value in a transaction, which leads to less need for a human to complete a transaction. Lost yet? I have two words for you that may spark a different mindset; self-checkout. Yes, this all ties back to Selflessness, hold on.

The internet has been a wonderful tool for countless reasons. With it, both time and money have been saved (ish) in almost as many ways. Now when we go to a supercenter, there are typically more self-checkout lanes open than lanes manned by an actual human cashier. What's even more exclusive are the online pick-up capabilities. Grocery stores are getting a solid piece of this action as well, devoting driving lanes specifically to online shoppers. All of this in the name of technological advances and modern capabilities. (Is it worth depleting our social graces?)

In addition to self-checkouts and online pick-ups, we can do a variety of other things without ever leaving the comfort of our home. We can shop for almost anything online or in an app, have carry-out food delivered, schedule virtually anything, gamble, see a doctor, stream tv/movies/music/ podcasts, chat, learn, work, etc. So many things at our fingertips and if we really wanted, it is quite possible that we would never *have* to leave the comfort of our homes if you did it all in a very well-planned method.

Where does the autonomy end? I'll tell you right now, it doesn't. Technology is advancing at a rate far greater than what most of us realize (and not as fast as others think). Machines, wireless capabilities, autonomous influence and the shear desire to rely on *something* else to complete our work for us rather than *someone* - has overpowered certain elements within the 1st world workforce. This is a trend that will only continue to grow.

We like to save time, money and resources when applicable. Businesses *really* like to save time, money and resources. All is well, until we look way down that path we're heading. It involves much less human-to-human interaction. Each interaction *should* therefore hold more value, since the interactions are more limited. However, the art of conversation is already well on its way to being lost forever.

This is where Selflessness comes into play. Machines are not taking over the world, nor will they any time soon. That's the good news. The bad news is, people do not value one another as we should. Pull your face out of your phone while you're walking down the hallway that has other people in it. Look into the eyes of the people you meet (if you can). Greet them, smile...be human. Life is already passing by so fast, value the humans you meet in it, not the very technology speeding it up even more.

The next time you are in a place of Hospitality (patron or employee), remember the value of your words. *You* are valuable, so make a valuable conversation. Have a meaningful transaction instead of a mundane transaction that may very well be replaced by an autonomous replacement someday. The future of our children and our children's children literally thrive on how we interact with one another *right now*, if it's not already too late.

Corporations will continue replacing employees with machines and autonomous efforts because it saves on wages, taxes, insurance, mistakes, supervision, discipline, vacation, sickness, gossip, time, and communication. Workplaces have been and will continue to adapt with technology, or they will become obsolete and fail. Those are paying jobs the future cannot hold. That is inevitable, but not out of control. Human interactions must be valued in an attempt to save humanity from turning into a mindless, autonomy-subscribed customer, waiting around to do the same damn thing everyone else is doing in the same way they do it.

The next time someone asks you how you are, give them a genuine answer, but ask them in return! Care about their response, because if you don't, then you may as well tell them you can't wait for them to be replaced by a robot. You can't wait for your children or your children's children to compete for jobs when technology has a firm grasp on jobs human interaction used to thrive on.

Your words have value. You have value. Share it with one another to ensure a world of humans does not simply turn into a mindless transaction. If it does, what's the point? Interacting with people via virtual reality? That is a path that leads to the deterioration of the human race as a whole.

I honestly feel like I went on a rant and need to say something before everyone thinks I am against technology. I am not against technology or the advances it has made or is making currently. There are several advantages as well as disadvantages. This was merely a way of describing the possibilities of what may come should we choose to be selfish with our time and how we choose to spend it.

Get to know your co-workers better, even if you do not get along particularly well with them. Remember that the people that you come into contact within your world are people too. They have their own problems, sorrows, beliefs, humor and hearts too. Open a door and hold it for someone. Let someone over in heavy traffic, because, they want the same thing you do; to get wherever they're going. Remember that Generosity is the gift that keeps on giving. Be kind, but firm when needed. Do not let someone take advantage of your Selflessness or Generosity but remember that mistakes will be made. You may set yourself up to get hurt but anticipate its predictability. Meet failure with understanding and Clarity and Patience. This, collectively, will all show that you have maturity and at least a little Wisdom to offer for those willing to observe and listen.

The Takeaway: Being Selfless is no easy task. It requires us to put our needs second to someone else's. We look past what we want in life and shift Focus off of ourselves. Being letdown is only a possibility if our expectations exceed realistic capabilities within given circumstances. As long as we are Patient, our Generosity should be recognized at some point and paid forward over time, just as we need to be mindful of someone else's Generosity and Patience. We must remember to stay human and be more human than human for the sake of the future.

CHAPTER 6

STARS AND STRIPES

DUTY & HONOR

du-ty & hon-or

NOUN

1. a Moral or legal obligation; a responsibility.

   "Serving your country fulfills a sense of **Duty**."

NOUN

2. adherence to what is right or to a conventional standard of conduct.

   "To stand next to the brave men and women of this country is both a privilege and an **Honor**."

Raising your right hand to swear an oath is one of the most Selfless acts a person can volunteer for. There are a number of reasons why people choose to serve a branch of the military and/or choose to protect and serve the community by becoming a police officer. (For the record, military and police are not the only jobs/careers out there that deliver Duty and/or Honor, but they will serve as the focal point for the sake of simplicity.) Each commitment is a sacrifice, not just for the participant, but for their friends and families as well.

Each member is affected differently and reacts according to their circumstances. The participant subjects themselves to leaving life as they knew it behind for initial entry training. This is a period that (typically) breaks a human being down to be reconstructed in a way that prepares us for high stress. We are put on a strict schedule that usually starts very early in the morning and ends late enough at night that when all is said and done, *should* give you enough time to zonk out for 7 hours or so. Rinse and repeat. This is a daily routine that is aided by a consistent diet, physically demanding activities, and ideally, no distractions such as internet, computers, cell phones, television, radio, etc. This process really gives your brain and your body the bare essentials to rebuild life in a way that demands our attention is spent in more prominent ways that do not rely on personal technology (within reason).

Anyway, for everyone within the participant's support group or closely affiliated with it, life goes on as normal, just without that person around. The occasional update via mail, phone call or rare video chat gives a reminder that your person is away for a while, but they are still very much going on with life. Sacrifices have been made all the way around. Families give up time with the individual willing to rise to the call. Friends give up their time with someone that impacts their lives one way or another. If there are children, they really have no choice in the matter, and they have to go on without truly understanding what is happening. All of this is fulfilling a sense of Duty.

The country and the communities in it absolutely need people to put on a uniform, without question. No matter how you may feel about the military or the police, they are both necessary. Without a military, we would most likely find ourselves in a world of chaos and militias. I have no doubt that other countries would fight for territory on our soil and life would be completely different. Without the military, one of a few scenarios are possible; 1. There is no police force because the world is already so chaotic and divided. The police would not have enough ground or organization to maintain presence. 2. There are police, but on a very limited scale. They would likely have higher expectations to fill because of a military absence yet lack resources to fulfill those expectations because of the overwhelming circumstances no military would Create. 3. There are only police, who band together to form a military of sorts anyway, basically re-inventing the original National Guard. They would have to fight on several fronts, both foreign and domestic, all in an effort to preserve life without a military. Oh, and unless the police trying to fill military shoes have a lot of experience in air defense or marine operations, our ports and air space are going to get overrun anyway. Like I stated already, life as we know it would be completely different.

All in all, the people that stand in uniform, whether they are sworn to protect and serve, or defend the country from enemies foreign or domestic, (we) did so with some feeling of Duty. You are worth protecting. Our communities and country are worth defending, protecting and serving. Doing so preserves our way of life and ultimately, our freedom to live as we do.

How about exploring a life without police? Well, this could most likely lead to a military dictatorship. I realize this may stir some unrest and disagreement, which is fine, just remember we are merely looking at possibilities, not examining opinions. Anyway, should a military dictatorship come to power again in our world, life would be somewhat different than we know it. The scale in which the military operates would need to be adjusted, likely absorbing current police assets and capabilities. That does not mean however, the same tactics would be used. Assuming the Army took over police responsibilities, the judiciary system, due process, sentencing, punishments, etc. would all change quite a bit. This would likely turn to re-writing the constitution so that the military could stay in power until certain terms are met for the peoples' best interests.

On a country-wide scale, our country would probably be really safe, with more restrictions. It's really hard to tell how it would play out, but if we can agree that life would be very different, then that's all that matters. What is really important to take away from this is the military and police each serve highly valuable purposes. Everyone that puts on a uniform with the intention of serving the people is displaying a sense of Duty to both themselves and their Morals. Every day they go out and do their job, they are contributing to keeping our communities safe. They are contributing to keeping our country safe. (For the sake of argument, all safer than what either could be)

The friends and families related to the individuals wearing either or both uniforms are also fulfilling a sense of Duty, just in a different way. The support of these individuals is vital to their success and overall well-being. Without (your) support, those individuals have an even more difficult task than what their job requires of them because it's on them to maintain Resiliency, Confidence and purpose all on their own.

With or without support, members of the military and police officers serving the people one way or another stand with Honor. As long as they have the Integrity to do the right thing, Respect their fellow man, serve with Selflessness and are Loyal to their cause, then they are among the most Honorable people we could ever know. Rare breeds to say the least.

As for the support groups in family and friends, keep doing what you do. Your roles are vital, no matter how much anyone on the outside does not understand or cannot see; You are not forgotten. If you're the one putting on the uniform, remember to not take your supporters for granted. Think of where you might be without them to back you up.

Fulfilling a sense of Duty is an obligation both to ourselves and the people that depend on us. Friend or foe, your uniform is a line on the field. Anyone that willingly crosses that line is subject to the reactions of whichever uniform is responsible for enforcing the rules. That is the call of Duty. Standing ready to answer the calls is an Honorable thing to do. Hopefully society Respects each uniform and does what they are supposed to do.

The ones that go above and beyond in the military and are recognized for their efforts, are usually recommended for awards. The Medal of Honor (MOH) is the highest military award the United States has to offer its service members. Such acts that have been awarded typically involve the recipient putting their lives into grave danger. Their heroism is the epitome of Selflessness and Integrity. They chose to put others before themselves and their efforts saved lives.

Some of the recipients did not survive their efforts, but their legacies live on, and always will. In moments of chaos, Clarity came to these individuals. They realized what had to be done and they did their best with what they had available to them, always demonstrating Resourcefulness. The MOH recipients' stories serve as top shelf examples of Honor and Selflessness. Without them and what they did, bad situations would have been worse. More people would have died. More people would have suffered.

This is not an attempt to dismiss any other acts that are Honorable, it is just a way to put it to scale, if you will. Honor starts with Honorable intentions. Merely standing ready to do what needs to be one is the very beginning of that scale. It is incredibly difficult to be a MOH recipient and I have little doubt that any one of them would wish for anyone to go through what they did.

The Takeaway: Duty and Honor often go together. Uniformed personnel especially can attest to this (or argue against it), but the fact of the matter is; It is dishonorable to ignore or even object a sense of Duty. You do not need to risk your life to be Honorable but standing with the intention of being Honorable is a great place to start.

BETWEEN A ROCK AND A HARD PLACE

DEFIANCE & RESILIENCY

de-fi-ance & re-sil-ience

NOUN

1. open resistance; bold disobedience

"People suppressed by harsh living conditions show **Defiance** in order to establish a more suitable way of life."

NOUN

1. the capacity to recover quickly from difficulties; toughness.

"Picking yourself up after being knocked down dozens of times will build **Resiliency.**"

Adulting in a nutshell; Taking everything life throws at you and still somehow managing not to pull your hair out or punch (many) people in the face. Life has a way of pouring stress on us when we already feel like we couldn't handle another drop. Bill after bill, flat tire after broken phone screen, after family death, after annoying cold, etc. (many of which come simultaneously or in rapid succession of one another). It's quite easy to feel overwhelmed by whatever we have going on, especially when uncommon variables are presently on our mind and in our conscious existence, like the things listed before.

Surely you've had a bad day, awful week, cruddy month, or even made it through an entire year stating you're ready for the New Year, so you can start over. Think about these things, what made your time Perceivably *bad*? Sickness, kids acting up, spouse acting out, wages, co-workers/management, ailment(s), separation/divorce, family/friend death, legal issues, etc.? It's your life, dig into what brought you down, especially over an extended period of time.

If you're stirring with emotions right now, good, hold onto them for a minute while we trudge through it. The "bad" things we allow to affect our attitudes ultimately make a significant impact on our decisions, which greatly affects results. Right now, you're (hypothetically) holding onto a memory of someone or something that "ruined" a period of time for you. You may have anger, sadness, Guilt, anguish, disappointment, etc. Agreed? If not, then you are either insanely positive and have no need to read my words anymore and the rest of the world could use some of your insight or you simply don't do well with being put on the spot thinking of a time when you were upset because that time is behind you and that's where it stays. Fine. Either way, we have to move on.

Take your memory, if you will, and do your best to put it into Perspective. This will require you to take a step back and try to look at the bigger picture. Who were all the people involved? What is the *core* issue? What lead up to the event? How did *everyone* react? How does everyone or everything stand now? What *good* came from it?

Ask yourself again, from the most unbiased standpoint you can muster: What *good* came from it? If you made a "What kind of stupid question is that?" face, I urge you to re-read Volume 1. Anyone that Accepts the question for what it is and is diving in, excellent job. There is positive to be taken out of virtually any scenario, yours included.

This takes a lot of Patience, Perception and maturity to Accept that things/people make mistakes *and* not hold it against them. It's quite easy to hold a grudge, burning a bridge because someone wronged you or someone close to you. Maybe the same thing or person has burned you several times. What makes it worse, is it's probably someone you care deeply about or want to care deeply about. How can someone hurt you over and over again? Why does the same thing keep happening?

Defiance and Resiliency, yes, hold on. Perhaps this is where Defiance may very well be a factor. Your feelings or ideology may be subjected to constant questioning because you are misunderstood, unappreciated or not Respected. It's hard to pinpoint, especially speaking generally, but it's really up to you to decipher why it is you may be facing similar situations repeatedly.

For the sake of Clarity, let's take a situation and apply it to an adult-child scenario. Assume that whatever memory you have been holding onto so graciously is now the mind of a child (if it wasn't already). According to Katherine Lee of verywellfamily.com, children may illustrate Defiant behavior when they "...may be trying to exert control over a situation or declaring her independence. He may be testing his limits and your authority. Or she may be expressing her dislike for something you asked her to do..." (2019)

Approaching almost any conflict or disagreement in this way has been surprisingly helpful even in adult situations. That's not to say adult situations are childish by any means, but rather a way of zooming out and looking at things from a more innocent standpoint. It's a way to defuse some volatile situations because if we are going to be the bigger person or adult in a given situation, it's helpful to Perceive the opposite party or object as we would a child, at least when it comes to identifying the reason for Defiance.

This is also assuming the memory you've been holding onto actually did something "wrong". Chances are, it was a mistake that can be avoided in the future or resolved with a healthy Balance of countermeasures to dissuade associated behaviors again. If you thought of a one-time scenario, it's okay because you never know when you'll be faced with similar circumstances again, but now you'll have a better approach to the whole thing because of your past experience.

That's the *good*. You went through the *bad* to learn from it. You have a more developed sense of appreciation because of it. You are the beneficiary of whatever hardship you feel you endured. You are the one building Resiliency, in this very moment. *You* chose to get back up. Now it's up to you to choose if you're going to keep moving forward while looking forward, or if you're going to stay right where you are, dwelling on what is done and gone, never to return.

The real question here is: What are you going to do with your time? Time is more elusive than we can consciously Accept. The older we get, the more we can look back on, the faster it seems time passes us by. It is in times that we are faced with Defiance that we must embrace the situations for what they are. Why may someone be wanting to exert control over a situation? Why would there be a disagreement and is it warranted? What is the best possible outcome? How do I want to spend *my* time?

It is in the moments that life knocks us down that we get to choose to get back up. Those moments are how we build Resiliency. The more we get knocked down, the better we get a picking ourselves back up. More importantly, we learn the ropes of life and eventually, it gets *really* hard to knock us around anymore. That's the point. That is what we should all strive for. Let your memory be just that, a memory. Learn from it so the next time you see the right hook coming, you know when to duck. Identify why you're fighting to begin with, so maybe you can defuse the situation before life comes barreling at you all at once just to knock you down again.

We can't prevent all hardships, however. Being sick or losing a loved one are almost inevitable. You can wash your hands and take precautionary measures to keep from spreading germs, but something will get to us eventually anyway. Losing a loved one is just a matter of time. Celebrate their life and the time you shared. Live on in a way to Honor them. Just try not to take every hardship as a negative occurrence. Find the positive and continue growing, no matter what happens.

The Takeaway: We're all going to get knocked around in life. The sooner we Accept it, the better. The sooner we can identify core issues of Defiance, the sooner we can meet them with our ever-growing Perception, ready to help turn the situation into something productive. No matter how much it hurts, life may kick us while we are down. Remember to get back up and move forward. Every time you do, you build your Resiliency, which is pretty damn awesome.

CHAPTER 8

DOWN THE RABBIT HOLE

MELANCHOLY

mel-an-chol-y

NOUN

1. a feeling of pensive sadness, typically with no obvious cause.

"Sitting in a state of **Melancholy**, he pondered
the point of his own existence."

Emptiness, sorrow, sadness, the dark places we can end up in when we experience one or more things that affect us in a negative way. The kinds of things we may not realize or consciously acknowledge until sometime later, if at all. There are a variety of reasons we may experience Melancholy, of which solely depends on the circumstances surrounding us at any given time. Getting into a "funk" is often unrealized by the victim, but others notice. Ideally, the better someone knows you, the more likely they are to notice your sadness. Of course, the more typically sad a person you are, the harder it is going to be for people to pick up on.

So why talk about Melancholy? Well, the first step to fixing a problem is identifying there is a problem. While we are working at enhancing our Perception skills, we must include more subtle, but very real issues that every human has faced, is facing or is highly likely to face in the future. Some people are more prone to these subtle issues than others, which is where the less susceptible folks can use the opportunity to apply what they have learned or want to inspire by helping a soul in need. We are all programmed differently, so your situations will differ from almost anyone else you can think of. Every interaction, every influence both direct and indirect, can make all the difference.

Without revealing names or obvious variables, someone close to me suffered from Melancholy as well as depression. Their circumstances superceded those of other people close to me as soon as they unfolded. The series of unfortunate events took their toll. While each one took something away, both literally and metaphorically. The physical absence of someone we love or not having something we once cherished can do unmeasurable damage to our will power.

Put yourself in similar shoes, if you can. Surely you have lost a loved one, or something with great sentimental value that could never be replaced. These are the more obvious things that contribute to our overall depression, but Melancholy is a bit harder to identify. Even after you have dealt with life as it fell apart before you and you have come to Accept reality, something still eats at you. Something deep inside you is still dark and empty. It lies in wait while you resume everyday life. Dormant like a volcano, smoke omits occasionally, foreshadowing the eruption to follow if you're not careful.

One of the best things you can do is sit down and put your thoughts in black and white, whether it be pen and paper or type them up. Brain dump whatever is going on inside you. Start with that very moment, acknowledging something is bothering you in the first place, or even better, Accepting it when someone else is trying to get you to take a grip on reality. Of course, this may be much easier said than done because you may be agitated with someone asking if you're okay or saying you are not acting like yourself. These are incredibly brief moments that are up to you to act upon productively. That's not saying that every single time you need to do this, but if more than a few people you know are taking notice, it's probably time you listened.

It is okay to be down, or off. It is nothing to be ashamed of nor something you should try to hide. It is human and talking about it or getting it out of your system in a visual manner is a great way to begin to deal with it, or deal with it more effectively anyway.

If you are not the one in a funk, be aware of those that are and try to get them out of it, especially if you would expect them to do the same for you. Try to acknowledge this action, whether delivering or receiving, as you could be the one failing to Accept, or deliver. Either way, look out for each other. The more open we are about what is bothering us, the more likely we are to be Respected for who you are and for being up front. This in turn should help others open up to you as well, which *could* lead to more stable relationships. Now, there are a bunch of different personality types out there. The "Supporters" typically will love this idea and wonder why it's not already a thing. Well, the "Analysts" are polar opposites of this mindset, and almost hate the idea of spilling their guts for people to see and help them pick up off the breakroom floor, because for 1, that's dirty and for 2, feelings just get in the way.

This is where everyone, no matter which personality type you may be, needs to be willing to compromise. Touchy-feely folks: know there are people out there that simply do not live their lives based on feelings. Number-people/analyzers: encourage the touchy-feelys to get to the point so they can relate to you a little better than before. Accept that there are people different than you and try to be human for 5 minutes. It's okay, because that's literally only .0035% of your day. Go ahead, check the math...please. I'll wait.

Seriously, giving someone the time to talk to you is worth so much more than you may realize and actually talking to someone is worth more than some of you may ever admit. The important thing to remember is being relevant. No one really wants to hear about ever single word of a conversation you're trying to recall with poor details and no real point, unless there's a punchline worth laughing at for longer than it takes for you to spit all the details out. If not, do yourself and whoever is choosing to listen to you a favor, and get to the point.

This may be an aggressive approach in a chapter about pensive sadness, but the reality is, we need to face it head-on. Stand your ground and acknowledge that life is kicking you while you're down and you deserve to know why. Clench a fist, grit your teeth, change your hair color, etc. and just know that you are going to get out of your funk. You *can* do it. You *will* do it. Then, be ready to help others get out of theirs. As time wears on, you can actually set your environment up for success. Be the positive factor that encourages others to face their problems and has the gumption to deal with issues by communicating *effectively*. Together, we can Create a positive and productive environment and being down will not be as big a deal as it used to be.

As a disclaimer, do not assume that someone that seems to have their life together is all sunshine and rainbows. Money, fame, assets, a "happy family", and other picture-perfect images does not mean an individual is not capable of being sad for no apparent reason.

Even the most Resilient of folks have bad days. Think of American Soldiers. Trained to be physically and mentally tough, Soldiers are some of the most unique beings on the planet. According to Kime (2019), "The military deaths reflect a national trend. In the U.S. the suicide rate has increased by 33% since 1999, and suicide is the second leading cause of death among people 10 to 34 years old." (para.7).

The main point is that even the ones that seem like they should be the strongest need help too. Do not be too proud, analytical, selfish or careless to think that you are above needing help, or above providing it.

The Takeaway: Everyone has down days, and they are absolutely okay. Talk about what is bothering you and deal with issues in a mature, well-communicated manner. This is the best possible way you and others will come to Create a positive, more productive environment together. Look out for yourself as well as others. You just never know when you may save someone's life without realizing it.

CHAPTER 9

HILL OF SILENCE

FEAR

fear

NOUN

1. an unpleasant emotion caused by the belief that someone or something is dangerous, likely to cause pain, or a threat.

"Saying you are not afraid does not
mean you truly have no **Fear**."

Darkness reveals doubt about your footing as you walk through an unfamiliar forest. Wind crackles through the branches of leafless trees and a distant howling sends a chill up your back, raising suspicion that someone or something is looming over your shoulder. A grip around your ankle sends you to the ground. Muddied hands prevent you from regaining Balance quickly. Your heartbeat quickens. Your breathing heavies. Panic and Fear stir within you as you fail to see what sent you to the ground. Branches snap behind you as a figure moves toward you in your helpless state.

The wind picks up, whistling through dark vegetation as it sweeps across the cold and muddy ground. You know you are their only hope, and now they are in more danger because you cannot get to them. The one person you love most may now be suffering the worst pain that either of you could imagine. You could have stopped it. You should have been there.

You try to offer yourself in their place. Panic, desperation, and helplessness are beginning to take their toll.

Before this gets any deeper, remember this is just a way to get into the headspace to discuss the topic at hand. This is certainly not an attempt to bring up feelings of Guilt, shame or real helplessness, but if it did, stay with me. Fear has a way of making us do things we do not necessarily ever want to do, often things we never imagined we would have to do.

The scene described before was merely a way to set the tone for the topic. If you are undeterred by creepy forests then I commend you for realizing you are not really in the hundred-acre woods. If you instead found yourself getting uneasy with the mentioning of the person you love most being subjected to harm, then the desired affect has been achieved. If you feel more sorrow because of any memories brought up, I sincerely apologize and ask you to reflect back further, putting a meaningful situation into hindsight. Think about what brings you Fear.

When we talked about Deception, I encouraged you to look under your bed. As a young boy, I remember thinking that someone could easily hide under my bed and await nightfall. They could either emerge while I slept or grab my ankles where I stood. No matter what they would choose to do, it was always a horrible imagination that ultimately had me jumping onto my bed and sleeping with my covers over my head. As a few days passed, my little brother proved my theory completely wrong when he hit me pretty hard with a toy whilst I was pretending my blanket was a suit of armor.

To my full disappointment and anxiousness, Fear set in even more as my imagination was flooded with demons and monsters hiding out under my bed waiting for me to fall asleep under my cotton and nylon armor. But this kind of Fear was purely in my imagination. To my knowledge, no demon or monster ever emerged from under my bed or closet and did anything to me (that I am actively aware of...kind of kidding).

As an adult, Fear takes on a different meaning. Focus shifts from childish things into more real-world situations. The more responsibilities we take on, the more likely Fear is to find its way into our lives in a much bigger way. If you have bills to pay, you may experience some discomfort when the due date was like four days ago and you already spent your money because you forgot all about the bill. Panic may set in for a few minutes, until you realize it's just rent, and the landlord is totally cool with you making another late payment. (Definitely kidding.)

How about those of you with big work assignments? Your department is relying on you, as is your team. You have management looking to you to deliver, and if it goes well, you could be up for a promotion. More stress than anything, but at some point, Fear has come across your range of emotions because you're human and you have contemplated the thought; "What if this goes horribly wrong?".

A big one for many of us with children is if something happens to them. Maybe it already has, and for those of you that applies to, I am terribly sorry. In a completely opinion-based position, to me, nothing could be worse than something happening to our children. Scratch nails on a chalk board while I'm cuffed to a chair, poke my eyes out, paper cut me between the toes, and make me listen to awful country music until I wither away completely. I'd much rather be the subject of torture than letting a child go through anything they do not need to.

Deep breath

Alright, Fear. We need to stay with that. Some people have phobias of very specific things. Others Fear things happening to them or someone they love. Fear is a tool for survival. Depending on how you are wired, trained and/or prepared, being afraid of something is natural. Your response, however, largely depends on who *you* are. For the sake of argument, let us look to nature to help identify reactions to Fear. A predator invoked by Fear is more likely to respond with an attack or "fight" than a prey, who is more likely to run away, "flight" or play dead "freeze".

Things you probably already know, fine. The real questions here are; What are you afraid of? How do you respond to Fear? If you really cannot think of anything you're afraid of, then you are either still very inexperienced in life or you are so experienced and Wise that you should be sharing your wisdom with others, which you probably are and it must be annoying when you preach to so many people and you know that most of them will not listen to you anyway and it's a constant battle as to whether you continue trying people to do certain things or not because you've seen some crazy stuff but they like, nah man, I gotta find out for myself and you all like, dude, I'm telling you it's not worth it, I've seen it a million times and then they like, calm down, bro, it's going to be alright but you know it's not going to really be alright and then they go and do the thing and come back like, man, I should have listened to you a long time ago and you all old and stuff now wondering when this sentence will stop.

Serious face. Staying alive is kind of important, and so is protecting the ones we love. The more your time and resources are in danger of being altered, diminished or taken away completely, the more you will probably Fear for a short while at least. It is the Fear that Motivates you to act. Facing Fear is the best way to defeat it. Plan affectively, of course. This is certainly not encouraging someone to go jump out of a perfectly good airplane without a properly packed chute, nor do I encourage anyone to play chicken with a moving train.

This is for more rational application. Bills can be late every once in a while, but do not let it become habit, from Fear of becoming evicted or without power/water/internet (no one forgets to pay internet!). Do your best on your work assignments. Give yourself the most time you can to work on it, eliminate all unnecessary distractions, Focus and get it done. Let a peer look over your work and give your constructive criticism. (You must be open to constructive criticism if you really want to prosper, not to mention it shows you have faith in whoever you are allowing to tell you what's jacked up, which may very well strengthen that relationship.) Address any deficiencies and continue mission. Oh, and failing is okay. It is how we respond to failure that makes all the difference.

Our children. Teach them the best you know how. Be there for them in every way you can be and is allowed. You also have to take care of you. Someone that does not take care of themselves is in no long-term way going to be able to affectively take care of someone else. Love is the single greatest thing we can give our children. Something could happen to them at any moment, just as it could to you. Accept it, prepare for what you can (within reason), and enjoy life as best you can.

Fear is a tool, nothing more. On a natural level, it is a tool for survival. On a corporate level, it is a tool to make you do whatever the institution wants you to do, often behaving in a specific way. On that note, I am going to give you something to ponder; What would religion be without the concept of Hell? Chew on that one for a while if you haven't already done so before.

The Takeaway: Fear is inevitable and frankly, it is necessary. We need Fear to react to situations naturally. We experience Fear in many different ways as we grow older. The more your Fears shift, the more you are growing or at least shifting Focus in life. You have a Perception that is still blooming, but Fear should always be a part of it. The same two questions will always remain in place that you should be able to answer at any time; "What are you afraid of?, And, How do you respond to Fear? What really matters is how you face Fear. In other words, don't be afraid to be in Fear, just don't let it rule your life.

CHAPTER 10

THE SUPERMAN

CONFIDENCE

con-fi-dence

NOUN

1. the feeling or belief that one can rely on someone or something; firm Trust.

> "He Accepted the challenge with great
> **Confidence** that he would prevail."

Fear is a tool for survival, but it is also used to control behavior and inflict doubt. It is used both directly and indirectly, sometimes on purpose and other times it is not intended. When we choose (or simply have no choice) to face what we Fear, an opportunity presents itself for us to morph into a stronger being. That stronger being that overcomes their Fear is sure to build Confidence to some degree.

We have all been there at some point or another, looking at the guy/girl we had a crush on, wishing we had the guts to say something to them. Or, stood up to a bully that pushed us around in school. Maybe it was standing up to our parents when they failed to have Confidence in us and what we were doing with our lives. No matter the circumstances, we have all had several opportunities to build our Confidence, as well as subject it to some serious tests.

Some of the qualities that make Confidence so great are similar to those of a reputation. Our reputations either back who we say we are or how others Perceive us. With that reputation comes some weight, if you will. Depending on how good or bad your reputation is, the weight you may have to "throw around" in the correct circumstances.

Take an old Western scenario, for example. Say an outlaw that has "Wanted: Dead or Alive" fliers posted throughout an entire territory. The outlaw has successfully robbed dozens of venues and killed several people in his wake, boasting a seven-man gang to accompany his crimes. Over the course of half a year, he has quickly become the most wanted man the territory has ever come to Fear. His reputation will continue to proceed him, as will his Confidence that he can continue doing what he does until someone stops him.

Enter the newly appointed Sherriff. A highly Respectable man of law with over twenty years of experience in various regions of a growing civilization in the Western world. He has brought down several criminals with various reputations, all with a common greed and disregard for those that got in their way or inconvenienced them in the slightest. Each criminal offered skill in either smooth-talking, gunslinging or fantastic riding abilities for their getaways. The Sherriff prevailed over all of them, thus building his Confidence with a concrete foundation. See how this works?

The Sherriff knows he has an experienced adversary with hardened criminals behind him, so he elects to deputize some men. He makes sure to bequeath what knowledge and Wisdom he can, preparing them for the inevitable shootout that is sure to take place in a matter of days. The Sherriff knows that Fear is a factor, that he assures them will help them stay alive when all hell starts breaking loose. For when Fear is at the door and Confidence (faith) answers, nothing worth Fearing will be standing before you.

This scenario could keep going, unfolding into a bloody shootout in a dusty town somewhere in Wyoming well over a hundred years ago, but how much could we take from that? The Sherriff may have defeated the gang, building the Confidence in his deputies and the town they defended, or them gang could have won this time, perpetuating their own

Confidence as ruthless villains. Either way, that was only going to be about Luck, circumstances and who had the better vantage point.

What we should take from this is Confidence is needed to face Fear and earned when the Fear is overcome. Think of a credit card, but for Confidence. A lender may extend a line of credit based on your history (reputation). In real-life, you are your own lender. It's up to you to lend yourself the Confidence you need to face whatever you need to face, when you need to face it. In an even bigger picture, maybe it's not about you. Standing up for something you believe in or for someone you Respect or admire are also motives to check the old Confidence credit line and see if it's time to increase the limit.

Building Confidence takes time, so be careful testing it every chance you get. Like our reputations, these things take a lifetime to build and only seconds to destroy. Do your best to prepare for situations you are certain you are going to face. Show Respect, have Integrity and be Trustworthy. Should you go into almost any scenario with this mindset, you are likely to be successful, thus adding credibility to your line of Confidence.

Oh! The Superman! Power posing is a thing, by the way. Our nonverbal cues such as posture, poses, gestures, etc. are all part of body language. Our body language has effects on both our self-Perception as well as how others Perceive us. Essentially, we have the ability to alter subconscious Perceptions through body language and facial expressions. Amy Cuddy (2011) published a video on power poses, where she found that participants who used a power pose before completing an assigned task, completed the tasks with higher Confidence than those that did not strike the poses.

Take this for as much faith as you will put into it. Try standing with your feet about shoulder width apart, straighten your back and hold your chin high. Put your hands on your hips and hold for about two minutes. With this stance, think positive, Confident thoughts. Own your Confidence, face your Fear and be triumphant in whatever you set your mind to. However, do not be deterred by failure. Remember that getting back up builds Resiliency, and failure is a way of learning something that does not work. Keep building on this mindset and you may Create an enchanting spell for inevitable success. (That one is for my Magic the Gathering friends our there ;)

The takeaway: Being Confident takes choosing Confidence before it is earned. The experiences we face are all opportunities in one light or another. Face your Fears to overcome them, but ideally when you are prepared to do so. Do not Fear failure, embrace triumph but be humble in the Confidence you build, before a bigger Confidence tests your Resiliency. Keep on Keeping on.

RESPONDEZ S'IL VOUS PLAIT

ACCEPTANCE

ac-cept-ance

NOUN

1. the action of consenting to receive or undertake something offered.

"Invitations to the party were sent looking
for either regrets or **Acceptance**."

This is an offer that you are either an advocate of already or are on the verge of responding to; Accept everything and everyone in life as they come. No matter how you are influenced by a particular noun, Accept it for what it is. Attempting to reject or deny someone, someplace or something, may only delay the inevitable.

It could be something you Fear. It could be someone you do not Trust. It could be somewhere you never want to be, physically or otherwise. Denying yourself the ability to first Accept life as it comes puts a pause on your personal growth and ultimately your Perception. We must change the way we look at things if we are to ever see something different.

Let's play a game. Use your environment to imagine shapes or images associated with one word. If you are in an office, you can probably use the drop-ceiling. If you are in your home, you can probably use a popcorn ceiling, or anything with a random design. If it is daylight and somewhat cloudy, use the clouds. If it is a clear night and you can see quite a few stars, you are fortunate. No matter which canvas is at your disposal, you now have a temporary mindset to see something different.

Let's get started. First up, use your canvas to imagine a face. Nothing fancy, eyes and a mouth. If you can see more details, that's great, if not, that is okay too. Wow, it's dark in here. Turn a light on if you need to!

If you can see a face, or multiple faces all around you, 1. Don't freak out. 2. Can you turn that image into a bowling ball? Add a Salvador Dali twist to it if you have to, the point is to morph the image into another image. Anything you want, but don't take too much time, because there is a bigger picture we are going to look at soon.

Alright, look at a face you imagined before and Focus on it. Will that face come to life and have a conversation with you? Gosh, I hope not. If it does, you may want to keep that relationship to yourself! Ideally, the stars, clouds, ceilings, designs/patterns, etc. are just that; stars, clouds, ceilings, designs/patterns, etc. Nothing more, nothing less. They each serve their purposes and exist through our own consciousness.

Everyone with semi-normal vision should be able to physically see a simple face in a mundane design. However, we should also first see the pattern for what it is first; A door, a wall, the ceiling, the sky. Most of these things we see every day and their initial value is a given. We Accept the stars as being stars. We accept clouds for being clouds. We accept our walls, floors and ceilings as walls, floors and ceilings. What else would they be? (Not actually asking.)

Now let's apply this Acceptance method towards people. Who is someone you do not get along with? Go on, there has to be someone that you either really do not like or at a very minimum, are completely neutral with but see often enough they come to mind. Focus on that person or group of people if that's what you need to do.

What is it about them that you do not like or disagree with? For the sake of ease, let's pick on Cowboy fans. (I know, how dare I?) / (The Cowboys annoy the hell out of me) / (Don't care about sports, so maybe he means a real cowboy?) Take Cowboys however you choose.

Anyway, you probably have an opinion one way or another whether it is supportive, neutral or against. Whether you have a position on either blue stars on silver helmets or gunslinging equestrians, it's just important to have *a* position.

Supporters: If you like the team strictly for the cheerleaders, you're not alone. If you have been a fan for several years, you probably grew up liking one of several likeable players. If you just like them for their uniform design, to each their own. If you care nothing about football and like real men, wearing leather boots with spurs, chaps, belt buckles bigger than my face, dusters and cowboy hats, then you have most likely been brought up on a farm or ranch by figures that fit a similar description. These guys are tough as nails and work long hours. The Old West is a distant memory, but never forgotten. Kind of like the Cowboy glory days, eh? (Please don't hit me.)

Neutral: You do not favor or oppose either football or dudes riding horses to do their jobs. You probably live in a city not located anywhere near Texas or Montana, and you get your coffee from a barista who makes you feel special every time she puts a smiley face next to your name on your "extra hot" latte. We get it, smiley faces are pretty special.

Against: Okay, New Yorkers, Cheese-heads and Eagles of the world, (purely being stereotypical for humor!) You despise Cowboys for one of several reasons. You're rivals, the Cowboys are a bunch of spoiled babies and/or you disagree with a hardnose way of life that fails to deliver an organic or nurturing satisfaction to your almond milk soy latte (Is that even a thing?!). Sorry, I don't know why I'm picking on coffee today, probably my own lack thereof! Despite your coffee preferences, Cowboys have rubbed you the wrong way at some point or another *or* a fan/advocate of theirs has. I actually grew up a San Francisco fan because I watched my first game as a kid, rooting against an old role model of mine, who happened to be a Cowboys fan.

Regardless of what we think of Cowboys, they are just that; Cowboys. Human flesh, active minds, families and friends. A Cowboy does his work and goes home to be with the people he cares about. (Definitely generalizing.) In the reality of things, if we had the opportunity to spend the entire day with a Cowboy, we would be crazy to pass it up. If they offered a Giants fan an entire day, all expenses paid, to do whatever they wanted, would they really turn it down? If you say yes, I think you need to ask your faces from earlier for a second opinion. Even a real cowboy moving cattle would be exhilarating in the right circumstances. Nothing like trying to re-create your own version of City Slickers.

Switch modes for a minute, what if your enemy attempted to make amends with you, offering something similar? A day together, all expenses paid where you could do whatever you wanted. Of course, this sounds like a trap. A professional sports player is not your enemy, (or maybe they are?) and are highly unlikely to ever make you feel intimidated or threatened.

Your personal enemy on the other hand, may very well be trying to Deceive you. This is where life can be tricky. You'll probably never Trust your enemy, but you should certainly Accept the possibilities of making amends with them, at least to get on neutral ground. No one should ever want to have enemies, but it happens. It happens more often than not, because we do not Accept circumstances for what they are, and some people hold grudges.

I understand having differences and not seeing eye to eye, believe me. It is not easy at all to swallow pride and Accept that another person/group of people think the way they do or believe what they do, but it is what it is, just as you are the way you are. The thing in common is that you both hold onto your views. Neither of you can make it to neutral ground without first Accepting these facts. Then a mutual Respect must be established, so that you can each have what is at your core, but without conflict.

Acceptance goes into every facet of life to some degree, even in rejection. Should you be on the side of rejection or need to reject someone or something, remember how it feels and make sure the recipient understands a reason. Disclose information about why there is rejection (if possible) and depending on circumstances, provide or point to an outline that could earn Acceptance. If you have been rejected, remember to continue building your Resiliency, Accept that you have been rejected and Respect the decision. If you are bound and determined to be Accepted, make sure you possess the qualities and traits required. Do not set yourself or others up for failure.

The Takeaway: We all have our views in life. Some of us like the Cowboys, some of us like being cowboys, some care about neither and others dislike the Cowboys but like cowboys. (Confused as I am?) The real point is to Accept circumstances and life for what it is. This is the critical step in life that allows us to properly identify a situation so that we can work towards a higher quality of life not just for ourselves, but everyone involved. Accept these words and you will continue heading down a path or greater Perception.

CHAPTER 12

MIND THE GAP

CLOSURE

clos-ure

NOUN

1. a sense of resolution or conclusion at the end of an artistic work.

   "We raised our glasses one last time while listening to his favorite song so that we could set the tone for **Closure**."

The end does not always seem like the end until we do whatever needs to be done to Honor circumstances. Closure is typically associated with relationships being brought to an end for a variety of reasons. Whether it be a breakup, separation, divorce, or death, Closure can incite a wild goose chase.

The more time we spend with someone, the more likely we are to absorb their personality and either mimic, compliment, despise, ignore or oppose it. In any case, it's really about getting an understanding of a given individual. This is most easily identified in schools and workplaces. We all have peers we mimic, compliment, despise, ignore or flat out oppose.

The less we get along with someone, especially if the feeling is mutual, the less of a feeling for Closure we will need. In fact, separating from those we do not get along with can Create a sense of satisfaction. It should go without saying, but the more we dislike someone, the greater the sense of satisfaction may be. It is important to understand this spectrum of Closure versus satisfaction so that we can develop a greater appreciation for the time we are spending with people in life.

We can rarely control who we go to school with, who we train with or who we work with. We cannot control who our family members are, so relationships there should always be built with a layer of mutual Respect at a very minimum. We don't always like select members of our family, and maybe it's mutual, but they're still family so a neutral relationship is still better than a negative one. (Not necessarily making any references to anyone in my own family!)

As for everyone else outside our family, we should still be able to identify relationships we enjoy and look forward to. Those people in our lives are most likely to have the greatest influence on our decisions, behavior and future plans. Essentially, we could argue that those people help make up who we are. To help support this claim, there is a somewhat popular quote out there that goes like this: *"You are the average of the five people you spend the most time with."* -Jim Rohn

Take that quote however you want, but in the end, I am personally inclined to agree. You may choose to include yourself as one of those people, as we are all our own person at the end of the day, no matter how much it may not feel like it. Consider the four people you talk to or at least spend time with the most during the week. Regardless of how much you like them or get along, the raw amount of time you spend with them or spend talking to them is what's important here.

I encourage you to write these names down on 4 separate pieces of paper and leave enough room to write down comments for each one. Comments for each name should have at least 3 things you enjoy and/or dislike about the person. Whatever sticks out the most as soon as you think of their name. Jot these thoughts down for each person and think about how much of an influence these people *really* have on you. Hopefully they impact you in a positive way. If not, maybe there is an insignificant impact, but you're stuck with whomever due to circumstances just outside your control or what have you. If they impact you in a negative way, Consider what you can do to productively counter whatever it is in their behavior or routines that drives you batty. Ultimately, this chapter is about Closure, no matter how much it may not seem like it right now.

We'll stick with those negative energies for now, stay with the name(s) and list(s) you came up with for them. Ideally, you should only have one (1) name in your life that has a *significant* negative impact on you. Mind you, this is purely my own opinion in which I have zero (0) research to back with. However, I will also argue that if you allow more than one person in your life to impact you in a negative way that you need to figure out how to change your life for the better, and sooner than later.

Anyway, negative energies, hopefully only one. These are actually opportunities for your character to grow and possibly do some good in the world. Nothing says the person who annoys you is a bad person, they just do things differently than you, which makes for a sand-filled gearbox relationship. Irritating as the whole thing may be, there is potential. If you can be kind, try to be understanding, Respectful and Creative, you could find a way to re-route your relationship into something less painful. Of course, this is assuming the person you deal with is not completely oblivious to the world and utterly incapable of grasping any other way of life but their own, which will require everyone to continue to work around them and their…bliss. If that is the case, I still encourage you to be kind and Respectful. Not everyone has the capacity to change and frankly, it may be better off if they stay the same.

Alright, moving on to the folks in our lives that help make us who we are. These people have an enormous piece of our attention, directly or otherwise. We may change how we say things, what kind of clothes we wear, the places we go, the things we want to do and eventually end up doing in life, because of these people. They have such an impact on us, they make up the very fibers of our being.

Quick challenge: Take a name away from your sight completely and imagine life *without* them, taken away right now. Seriously, take the time to do this. Let it sink in and come back to this later.

Well, I tried it and my heart is quite heavy. That person has a huge impact on me. Even I am almost at a loss for words, but that would leave this whole thing hanging. We need the *Closure*. The person you chose is most likely to be a best friend and/or family member you love and Trust. If it is a child, I would say that makes this even heavier.

Whoever it is, remember how you felt when you tried to picture life without them. What was the last thing you said to them? What was the last thing you did together? Do they know how you feel about them and is it mutual? The questions could go on and on if they were taken away at any given second. If they were, then what? Unless you already knew their time was coming or you already treat every time you see each other like it's your last, then the odds are you will face a giant void. It will be you and your thoughts. Memories colliding with a roller coaster of emotions.

As you stroll down memory lane, you will dig up the awesome times you had, the bad times where you regret your immaturity and all the times in between. This is your brain working to make sense of what just happened. This is your soul trying to cope with a new reality that you now have no choice but to face. That new reality is something you are probably not going to do well with, as a gap just found its way in between you and your grasp on life.

People respond to loss differently. Some turn to support groups like mutual friends/family, some withdraw from socializing at all, some may turn to alcohol and/or other substances (in attempts) to numb the pain. Others may alter their behavior completely, never to return to who they once were. There are several other ways people respond to loss in more positive ways, like dedicating work or Creating something to Honor memory. Depending on where we are in Accepting life as it has come, some situations may be easier than others. Either way, this is a lesson neither of us are about to forget.

That person *will* be gone someday. Whether it is before or after you likely remains to be seen. Until that happens, live life in a Respectable way with an open Perception for those that are different than you. This is in no way suggesting you should change who you are, unless you're disrespectful and narrow-minded, which I strongly doubt since you're reading the 2nd volume of Hindsight. (High-5 or 4 for you! Yes, that was for you specifically, Dan!)

Anyway, it's a bit more common for us to imagine our lives without someone we look forward to seeing or talking to as often as we like to. It's even easier to picture our lives without the ones we do NOT want in our lives, as we imagine it being so much better. What (I feel) many of us fail to do is Consider what life would be like for the ones *we* leave behind. Let that thought sit with you for a minute.

What kind of an impact have *you* made? How do people treat you and why do they treat you the way they do? What did you do to contribute to the lives of others?

I sincerely hope these are questions you take seriously. Life is what we make it. We are impacted by several people, but very few have a lasting impression that we are either subjected to regularly. The simple way to look at life is through our own eyes. The Perceptive way is to see it from someone else's point of view.

There is nothing we can do to avoid death. We have one (1) life (as far as we can prove scientifically). This is our one shot at experiencing anything and everything that comes across our radar. We spend time with people and either we enjoy them, or we do not. A more important question is whether they enjoy us (you) or not? Is our time well spent? Will we regret not doing something with or for the person who are a part of the list that makes us who we are? Are you ready to lose one of those people? Are any of those people ready to lose you?

Hopefully, you are never ready to lose anybody like that. It is better to have lived and loved than to have lived and never loved at all, as one could argue that is not living at all. The point to gaining Closure is finally Accepting that life has changed, which is okay…that's part of life. What happened, happened and there is nothing anybody can do to change it. Move on in a way that Honors memory, and just never forget what you had. Share memories with mutual friends. Pass them on to people that will enjoy and cherish your memories as much as you can expect them to.

The Takeaway: A major part of gaining Closure is Accepting what has happened. If you are in a situation you need Closure for, pain is inevitable, so brace yourself as best you can. Talk to someone, no matter how much you do not want to talk. It's okay to be down, just don't let life keep you there.

CHAPTER 13

THE THIEF OF LIFE

GUILT

gilt

NOUN

1. the fact of having committed a specified or implied offense or crime.

> "The underlying feeling of **Guilt** was a warning to his soul that he had done something wrong."

We've heard the expression, "Guilty conscience" at some point or another in our lives, or if you have not, then you will. It is a statement often associated with a wrongdoing to some degree, or at least the Perception that wrong has been done. For the time being, we will Focus on our own feelings of Guilt. Surely there has been a time when you did something that you probably shouldn't have, then had some feelings of remorse. Maybe you were mad at your little brother/sister when you were kids, so you slammed your door in their face trying to get away from them.

At the time, it was a reaction to their annoying, clingy behavior. They followed you around everywhere, mimicking your actions, interests, etc. They were awful at being us and they could never be as cool as us, so we were annoyed they even made the attempt and their very presence irritated us more and more…by the way, this is just a generalized example. If you either had no siblings or loved your siblings for nothing less than who they were, please bear with the scenario as we move forward. Hopefully, you can think of someone that closely represents the feelings we are trying to tap into.

Moving forward, the siblings that antagonized us on the regular were looking up to us because we served as one of their most influential people in their lives. We provided a very early representation of a male/female figure in which they would watch us closely and either agree with and love or disagree with and despise. (It's not either/or, but rather a spectrum of relativity.) Again, we will stick to the side that we served as the role model in this case.

Years down the road, you and your sibling(s) have grown up and gone down your own paths in life. Maybe you have kids of your own now, and as you watch them do things in spite of each other, you may begin to think about when you and your sibling(s) were kids. It's not until we look back at pictures or reminisce distant memories of our siblings and realize how awful we could be to them.

They followed us around like lost little puppies. They tried to like the things we liked, whether they understood it or not. They tried to act like us, talk like us and dress like us. They annoyed the holy hell out of us, and we wanted to kick them across the room.

We were their idol. We were the one they looked up to. We treated them like dirt because our own selfishness and incapacity to indulge their innocence or genuine curiosity let us believe they were a burden. We were the truly awful ones.

If you do not feel bad about kicking someone away from you or out of your life when they really needed you, there must be more to it. Not everyone's circumstances will align but for the most part, we have all had *someone* in our lives that looked to us for guidance, support or even basic friendship. If you have been a perfect sibling, supporter, friend or what have you, please, tell the world how the hell you did it.

For the rest of us that are more human, a feeling of Guilt may have been brought back into light with this conviction. (It has for me.) This may be a good time to reflect on the actions we took back then. How did we treat the people we love? Was our insolence truly justified? Where are our relationships with those people now? Is it too late to improve the relationships that need it?

These are just a few of the questions we should ask ourselves, even from the small moments in our adolescent years, because frankly, they are more important than we may realize. Do yourself a solid and the people you may have wronged, even if it was just Perceivably, and reach out to them if you can. It doesn't matter if you talked to them yesterday, last week, a year ago, or 10 years ago. Reach out. Life is too short, and if you are going to be a Respectable member of society, let the people that do or should matter have some dignity and maybe even provide Closure for one if not both of you.

Guilt is like a ball and chain. The more Guilt we carry around, the heavier we feel and the harder we have to work to get through life. If we give ourselves or others the opportunity to square things away or make sure we're good, then you are taking a responsible step towards being that role model that was looked up to. Even if they hurt you or failed to meet your expectations, remember that people are human and make mistakes. You too will be looked up to one day if you're not already, and you're going to make (more) mistakes. Bear that in mind as you think of your own role models.

Alright, Guilt is not all about influencing others. We can inflict Guilt upon our own conscience. Sometimes we do things we *know* are bad, but we just can't seem to help ourselves. Whether it is because we believe we deserve punishment, or simply do not care about what happens to us, chances are we are carrying around Guilt of some kind. It can literally feel like a blanket filled with lead. We drag it around with our bucket of doldrums, looking at the things around us with a grey behind our eyes.

It might be fair to state that Guilt and Melancholy can be related, depending on our circumstances. The point to overcoming both is addressing the issues in our life that may be weighing us down. We have to identify what is going on or what has happened. If we don't first acknowledge all the possibilities, then figuring out a long-term solution is going to be impossible.

Guilt may very well be an underlying feeling, especially if we have yet to fully realize how we may have affected someone or ourselves. We have to Respect ourselves before we can Respect others, so take that how you need to. As long as we are Respectable and can take the time to identify the factors bringing us down, then we may be able to work on Acceptance, which helps build our Resiliency. Of course, if it is us that was at fault, then we must show Selflessness and Integrity before we can begin fixing whatever it is we broke or helped break. Enter Motivational quote here:

"Mistakes are always forgivable, if one has the
Courage to admit them." -Bruce Lee

The Takeaway: No one should ever enjoy feeling Guilt, but it is inevitable for us humans. Guilt is the soul's way of saying, "Hey, you probably shouldn't have done that, but you did so I'm going to keep sitting on you until you make it better." Be Respectable and have Integrity. It is okay to make mistakes, so long as we learn from them and acknowledge and make amends with the people that may have been hurt along the way, including ourselves.

CHAPTER 14

SWISS ARMY KNIFE

VERSATILITY

ver-sa-til-i-ty

NOUN

1. ability to adapt or be adapted to many different functions or activities.

> "His ability to change gears between challenges is a great example of **Versatility**."

Five syllables, I know. If you just counted them out like I did just to make sure, cheers! Six syllables if you say it in pig Latin (I think?). I don't know for sure, but hey, let's get those gears shifting.

Having a strong ability to Focus on your objective is essential for Versatility. Life is a journey made up of an infinite number of paths for us to travel. Some paths lead to the same place while several lead to many other places. It is your life, the paths you choose are solely on you (as long as you're a legal adult and are not barred to other kinds of restricting factors). However, there are many factors that contribute to the paths we choose such as family, friends, resources available, education, finances, and future goals both short-term and long-term.

Now, depending on what your overall goal in life may be, you may be met with more resistance *or* support than others. We just talked about

Closure and how difficult life can be without someone we really look up to involved in our lives every day. This is where Versatility and Selflessness come into play. Versatility on your behalf, and Selflessness on whoever you need it from most. That's not to say you don't also need to practice Selflessness, but we'll get to that in a minute.

Assume you have a lifelong dream to work doing something you love. The path that you are required to take just to get to the door may force you to leave your friends, family and everything familiar to you, behind. The younger you are, the more ideal this situation *should* be. College, trade schools, joining the military or foreign service or what have you are all routes widely accepted among American culture (not necessarily joining the military unless you or your family already has military ties, bear with me).

The people that matter most in your life are probably more likely to help you along your way to continuing your education or developing skills at a younger age than if you were to stick close to home and say, take up the family business or trade. There is absolutely nothing wrong with this, except it isn't for everybody. Doing something just because it is assumed you will do it or because it is what is expected of you does not mean that is what you are interested in or destined to do for the rest of your life. Obligations like this can impose a heavy weight when Considering which courses of action you take in life.

The greater the expectations and the more you are relied upon to fulfill obligations like these, the harder it is to break free of ties that may be holding us back from achieving the things that will make you happy. That's not to say the obligations or expectations are not legitimate due to whatever the circumstances may be. However, if the people that have these kinds of influences in your life really love you and support you for who you want to be, they will do their best to help you along your way. It's that simple. Versatility comes into play when you recognize how people depend on you and what you contribute, and if you are sensitive to their needs. If you can help those people figure out how to accommodate for your absence, then you are acting with an admirable dose of Selflessness that should be Respected. This demonstrates a level of maturity as well as a sense of Duty that you are committed to relieving as best you can. This does not mean others are responsible for *your* needs, rather, you are accountable for them and how it is you get what you need in life.

If you want to be a Versatility beast, you take on multiple obligations at once. Maybe you already do, maybe you do it because you have no choice. You may have a job, go to school and have no one you rely on directly to help you get along in life. Maybe you have kids, work and do not get much support from others. No matter your circumstances, those of you that switch hats throughout the day are probably very Versatile. Your efforts are admirable, even if they seem unappreciated or go unnoticed for a period time.

Your hard work speaks volumes about your character and determination. Someone looks up to you, whether you realize it or not. Being able to change hats early and often, and *well* is incredible, but it is also exhausting. Like a well-oiled transmission, changing gears is one smooth transition after the other. Shifting allows distribution of power into the right kind of energy the motor needs to cater to whatever gear it is in.

In our lives, our motors are all different. We fuel ourselves differently, we shift differently and for different reasons, and we take care of ourselves differently. You may chalk the term motor up however you need, whether it be your mental state, spirituality, physicality, emotional well-being or what have you. The way we run and refuel are critical in how effective we are at completing the objectives before us.

Fueling yourself with things like sugary energy drinks, salty snacks, *negative energy*…you may get fired up really well for a short amount of time, but you will not sustain energy for very long and you *will* crash. Fueling like this is detrimental to your Versatility and long-term sustainability. Not knocking on energy drinks or salty snacks, as I love each in moderation. Negative energy on the other hand can be hard to digest. Unless you are keen to turning negative energy into positive, I strongly suggest denying as much of it from entering your life as possible until you understand how to not let it affect you in a negative way. Let me say this again, completely unrelated to Versatility because this alone is bigger than being Versatile: *understand how to not let it (negativity) affect you in a negative way.*

Things we subscribe to in life purposely or otherwise influence our decisions and can alter the paths we take or try to take. Some things inhibit decisions, thus speeding up our process. Hopefully we are prepared for

those moments or have the ability to adapt quickly. Anyway, regardless of timing, do your best to moderate the things you allow into your life. Until you have a solid base of Versatility, take one situation at a time and digest it for all its worth. Learn from your mistakes as well as those of others. If you can do this at a minimum, you can build a foundation of Versatility, whether you choose to change gears like an Indy car racer or cruise through life on autopilot. The difference between you and everyone on cruise control will be your ability to switch to manual if you want or have to.

The Takeaway: Honestly, Versatility is not for everyone, nor is it entirely necessary. It's up to you if you want to live life like a Swiss Army Knife, being equipped to complete several diverse tasks without depending on someone else to do them for you. If that's not for you, it doesn't have to be. No matter how you run your motor, remember that dealing with negative energy in a positive was is one of the most important ways we can keep ourselves burning clean, positive energy.

CHAPTER 15

IT IS WHAT IT ISN'T

CREATIVITY

cre-a-tiv-i-ty

NOUN

1. the use of the imagination or original ideas, especially in the production of an artistic work.

"Her mix of pastels and emotion illustrates raw **Creativity**."

From a very young age, curiosity leads us to explore things we do not yet understand. Some things are innocent and do not go anywhere because some of those things do not pique our interest for very long and we move onto something that does. It's that same curiosity that possesses some kind of desire to be filled, one way or another. Whether it be spent trying to figure out how to get the circle in the square, where to put your next "X" or "O", or what to make to make yourself to eat with minimal groceries, curiosity is the base of our Creativity.

We are all curious about different things. This becomes more apparent as we get older and we notice, gaps, if you will, between our interests and those around us. Some of you do not notice any gaps because you do exactly what you like to do in life and are surrounded by people that enjoy the same things you do. For those of us that are not so fortunate, we seek to fill those gaps through many trial and error methods.

We may find ourselves branching out to people we see have similar potential or that have similar interests. We may find ourselves trying new things or explore places that we had only previously Considered before. As we test the boundaries, we can continue refining our own. Much like applying a medium to paper or a canvas, we may only have an idea of what we want to put down, but do not quite know how we want to apply it, so we experiment.

Depending on the results of our experiments, we will either continue using the method we believe is working for us, or we will scrap it and try something new. Either way, it is important to realize our actions and whether they are getting us closer to or further away from where we want to be. Are we Creating what we want in our lives? Do we have the right tools to even do what we want? These are a couple of the most basic questions you need to ask yourself before you try to build a house (or anything else super constructive) with bubble gum and paper clips. Fun point, if I may: take the term "house" and put it into Context. Did you envision a human size house with a door in the front with 2-4 windows? It's okay if you did, but the term may take on several different parameters. One could absolutely build a "house" out of bubble gum and paper clips; it just might be very small. The house could be for a pet gecko, we don't know. Or if you wanted to be super Creative, one could construct a small home that is human size by using a literal ton of bubble gum and a couple million paper clips. Also, I am going to bet that you're assuming the bubble gum is *chewed*. Again, not necessarily the case, but it is a fun to ponder the possibilities as well as the improbabilities.

Our imaginations may have run wild when we were younger, until we started gaining education. As we learn about the things that intrigue us, we develop an appreciation for what it is. That does not mean it will continue to intrigue us. Apply that to literally anything you have taken an interest to in life. The more you learn about someone, someplace or something, the greater an *appreciation* you have for it/them. That means you have learned more about what it really is, and hopefully you are figuring out whether that is what you want/need in your life.

So how does figuring this stuff out tie to Creativity? Well, that's ultimately for you to fill in. Creativity does not apply strictly to artistic circumstances. One can be Creative in the way they speak, fight, parent, argue a point, etc. One could also argue that everything we do is a work of art, but that is beside the point.

The real prize of Creativity is when you can achieve or help achieve a work of art that you are proud of. It doesn't matter if you scribbled lipstick all over your face to scare an ex away for good, or rigged a couple 2x4s to make your own tv wall mount, the point is to Create something in life that you are proud of or can fill a level of satisfaction. It also means doing it within your means. Good Creativity does not (often) come from well-financed operations. This is solely an opinion of my own and I will elaborate.

Without striking too many chords, let me first say there's nothing wrong with well-financed ops. This is more geared towards those who are not as fortunate and may be in need of some reassurance that it's okay to not have a bunch of resources available. This chapter should pair nicely with Resourcefulness, as several people struggle to manage to get through life with what they have. It's good Creativity that sets us apart from the mundane, run-of-the-mill folks that take what they're given and expect more to be handed to them. We have to learn to appreciate the things we have, Respect what we are given and Create positivity with what we can. That's it. If you have the resources and can just pay for the exact things you want in life, more power to you, but I'd venture to say your Creativity is taking a hit.

A more influential approach is to achieve positivity through exchanges in either goods or services. There may come a time when currency is not worth a damn thing, and a new void will need to be filled. Maybe clean water or rich soil will become the currencies of the world and unless you will know how to harvest either, you will have to find something you're good at that others are going to have a demand for. Even if currency does not collapse, you may still find yourself in a situation where you are fighting to offer something someone wants in exchange for something you need. No head in the gutter references intended.

No matter which way you choose to navigate through life, know there are people out there fighting for things they want and need. Never judge someone for the path they are on, as you probably have no idea where they came from, or where they're going. If they are on a path that will land them (or others) in danger or trouble, do your best to apply guidance where applicable. Otherwise, keep on living a life of Morality, be Resourceful, Respectful and never be too quick to dismiss your curiosity, because your Creativity depends on it.

The Takeaway: Curiosity is the base of Creativity. If you deny your curiosity to run its course within reason, then you stifle your own Creativity and you subject yourself to becoming another average Joe or Jill, following the rest of the followers as they go through the motions of life. If that's all you want to do, that's fine, but always use your blinkers and stay out of the fast lane when the rest of the world wants to pass you.

CHAPTER 16

FUELING THE FIRE

MOTIVATION

mo-ti-va-tion

NOUN

1. the reason or reasons one has for acting or behaving in a
   particular way.

> "As soon as the love of his life walked into the
> room, he felt a sudden burst of **Motivation**."

Do you remember being very young or recall watching a young child that
would "show off"? Someone new came into the room or they discovered
something new and wanted to share something they are/were enthused in
with whoever they could. Either they wanted to see if it also piqued their
interest as well, or they desired attention so they could gain Confidence
that what they thought was cool, really was cool. The energy tied to their
actions is underlined with Motivation.

Mind you, I did not say their actions were appropriate, or otherwise
defined. The irony of getting older is that we gain knowledge and experience
with every passing day. There is literally nothing you can do to stop yourself
from gaining any kind of experience, unless you are no longer apart of the
living. Even then, who is to say we stop learning? Anyway, the older and
Wiser we get, the less likely we are to be impressed by something we have
seen time and time again.

This can be illustrated with a simple example: Imagine a young child you know. They want to show you the trick they just learned. They pretend to grab your nose and "steal it", thus putting their thumb between their fingers and taunting you with their favorite new line: "I got your nose!". They are so sweet and innocent, they cannot get enough of this new trick, so they do it to you say, six more times. You are happy to oblige, until you feel the newness wear off much faster than they do. Before you know it, they've stolen your nose 17 times, never gave it back, but the damn thing keeps growing back and they're right there to steal it over and over again.

Can you imagine? That child was so excited to be there with whomever they felt comfortable enough to steal their nose 17 times, nothing else mattered to them. Those few moments Created a memory and potentially satisfied a level of experience critical for that child's development. It may not seem like it but indulging in curiosity allows thought processes to play out, which should in-turn allow development towards who we are going to be.

If you have been subjected no nose theft time and time again, allowing curiosity to flourish, kudos to you. There may not have been much evident Creativity from our Perception, but to them, it was their world in those few precious moments. You may have very well served as a vital block for building someone's Motivation. That my friend, is a very powerful thing.

Children stealing noses are not the only examples of generalized Motivation. The way we are brought up will likely serve as a template for what Motivates us, stemming from a few key factors such as attention, finances, status and education. These factors are definitely affected by the amount of each we do or do not receive in life, thus causing us to act in ways that get us closer or further away from how much we want of each.

Sometimes those actions are positive. Graduating high school/college, getting married to someone we love and Trust, starting a successful business, making an impact on the community that inspires others, etc. Sometimes the actions are not so positive. Failing to complete school or get a job to make our own money, turning to addictive substances, being violent or untrustworthy, or participating in unhealthy relationships, etc.

No doubt about it, our actions and behavior are all tied to what Motivates us. Some things are very basic and adult-like, such as making sure bills are paid so we can play video games. Parents strive to make sure their children are taken care of while others may work on self-preservation and long-term goals. No matter where you are in life, you should think about what Motivates you. I'll venture you can sum the most influential factor up with one of the following five words: Family, friends, finances, future or freedom. Nothing says you have to have one of these factors at all, nor does it only have to be one. One could very well be because of the other, it all depends on your life and the circumstances both within your control as well as out of your control. The important thing to remember is Focus on what matters most and work toward it.

Back to the child aspect really quick. You were a child once, I'd safely assume. Can you remember a time that you were excited to share something and the person or people you shared with did not react the way you imagined? Especially when it was in a negative way. This is probably a "yes", unless you never had any expectations ever, then you are a Resiliency master. For everyone else, what did the unfulfilled reaction do to your self-esteem? More importantly, how did *you* react?

As children, we had a harder time accepting adult concepts and reactions because we did not yet have the capacity and/or experience that would prepare us for such things. Those moments in our life that did let us down were still valuable, we just did not like them as much as the times we stole someone's nose 17 times so we could move on to something better the next day. We were Motivated to either continue on with our fascinations, or we were discouraged because we had a hard time keeping the people that mattered most interested in what we were interested in.

True value can be found in few different ways, one of them revolves around us having support in all we did growing up and we are not pressured to choose something to be Passionate about because we simply do not have to worry about where life might take us. Another way is to have neither support nor discouragement, thus leaving us to figure life out for ourselves, resulting in a lot of trial and error/observing/mimicking others as much as we can. And finally, we were discouraged from our interest(s), rarely supported if ever, refining our own love of whatever subject at hand. If we were truly Motivated and Passionate about it, then we stood our ground no matter how much resistance we encountered. Watch out for these individuals to make a hell of an impact when they're Motivated. They had to earn their stripes from the very beginning. There's nothing against those that received all the support in the world or neutral support at best, but the ones that fought resistance will hold onto their Passion a lot tighter than someone that didn't have to fight for it or someone just trying it on because they're still unsure. Like I said, Motivation is a very powerful thing. Motivation in the face of Resiliency is even more powerful.

You may want to say I'm wrong or you disagree, and that is awesome! That means you have had a personal experience that suggests otherwise, which is perfect. This isn't about right and wrong for me, it's about what is right for *you*. Whether you agree with me or not is fairly insignificant. What is important is that you at least *understand* what I'm trying to get across and it gets you thinking about what Motivates you, which allows you to plan your life with greater accuracy than before, that's all.

Some of us may find it quite easy to say what Motivates us, but there will be those that do not have such an ideal time picking it out because they're still trying to make their way through life. That's absolutely fine, it isn't a race. It is your life, in your hands (generally speaking). If you are unsure of what Motivates you or are even curious to participate in an exercise that may help legitimize your beliefs, start by making a list of things that make you uncomfortable. The things on your list should have some things in common such as large groups of people, numbers, children, outside/inside, music type, money associated, activity associated, etc. Try to find a common denominator so that you can sum up things you do not like for sure, in a more generalized sense. Then make a list of *opposites*. Things you enjoy, followed by finding a common denominator for those as well.

The results are there for you to ponder and question as you see fit. The next thing you should do is question how much of your life is aligned with what you enjoy. This may open up a whole can of worms, but it will be worth it if you harness Motivation to do something about it. Whatever you are Passionate about is worth your time and Consideration. Even if you cannot act on something you are directly Passionate about, surely you can find something closely related.

Finding Motivation to do anything in life takes time and energy, but if we are doing something that Motivates us, it doesn't feel like it. Coffee is a Motivator for me. Start small and work your way up to completing daily goals, which should help chip away at weekly goals, which contribute to monthly goals, so on and so forth.

For the record, Motivation is not always a comfortable thing. Adrenaline induced by Fear is also very real. Being chased by angry rottweilers or being screamed at by three drill sergeants at the same time are good reasons to be Motivated to move your butt with a purpose. Putting ourselves in danger is not a positive way to gain Motivation, but it happens every day. I sincerely hope people can find more constructive ways to seek Motivation, as putting yourself in harm's way is also endangering someone else one way or another. Please bear that in mind as you move forward, not just for yourself but for others in their journey through life.

The Takeaway: Motivation is a very powerful thing. It is as simple as that. If we can figure out what Motivates us, then we can ideally plan our lives accordingly. We are also highly likely to tie our Motivation to whatever it is we are Passionate about. If you are in a place or can get to a place where your Passion perpetually fuels your Motivation and vice versa, then you are doing a hell of a job at life. Hopefully your Passion contributes to society in a positive way so as to inspire others that they too can unlock the Motivation-Passion loop. (Officially calling this the Mo-Pa loop.)

CHAPTER 17

OWLS ON OVERWATCH

WISDOM

mo-ti-va-tion

NOUN

1. the quality of having experience, knowledge, and good judgement;
    the quality of being Wise.

> "Knowledge speaks to answer questions
> while **Wisdom** observes and listens."

A bit of a convicting moment there, typing that example sentence. How often do we really stop and *listen* to another? How much Confidence do we place in someone else to inform us with unquestionable expertise? Of course, it's a catch-22. One cannot go through life without questioning others or even themselves and expand to expand their own curiosity or knowledge base. What I believe inhibits true Wisdom is to listen to others, take what they have to say into Consideration, and form your own Perception based on everything else *you* have to offer.

Pretend you have the ability to put every ounce of your own defined Wisdom into a bottle, right now, a potion if you will. You would simply be duplicating everything and not losing any of who you are. How much would your potion be worth? Call it $1 per year you are old. Add another $1 per grade you completed in school. Add $5 per degree you have earned. Add $1 per major life-changing event you have experienced barring the schools, this would include things like children, marriage, major purchases, career choices, etc. Obviously there are many more things to take into Consideration, but these few things should set a decent base price with the assigned variables.

If you have done the math and exceed $50 for your potion, I want one. Mine does not exceed that price range (yet), but I look forward to the day that it breaks that mark. If we really wanted to get super technical, we absolutely could. However, we can't really make our own Wisdom potions so at this point, it's really about figuring how much we believe our Wisdom is worth and if we are satisfied or not.

What's that quote?

"Better to remain silent and be though a fool than to speak out and remove all doubt." -Unknown

This is one I ponder quite often. It's easy to remain silent (for some), allowing others to make their way through life however they can. Mistakes are made, successes are wallowed. The irony in gaining Wisdom is that it is a concoction of knowledge *and* experience. Sitting back and only observing may help one gain knowledge, to an extent, but it hardly does anything to satisfy experience.

Sitting back and not taking action has a price attached to inexperience. It may be the safer road, but it does not get you any further than you can see. If you have a limited Perception, then your vision is limited at best. One cannot assume they have a clear sunny day to look miles down the road unless they are able to clear their skies of cloudy judgement and bring in positive vibes to light the way. It's your journey, travel by day with Clarity of vision to gain the experience you need in order to earn Wisdom. Question people, places and things in life that are on or near your path. It is the best way to expand your own knowledge, enhance your Perception and get others to hopefully do the same.

Time for Closure: No matter where life leads you, remember to be Selfless and Accepting. Respect is key to achieving mutual understandings, no matter where you're are on agreeing or disagreeing with others. Allow Context to flow freely as you Focus on Clarity. Balancing Passion with Intellect and Integrity will allow us to avoid Deception and Liability. Be

Resourceful as you are met with obstacles, have Confidence that you will overcome them with a sense of Creativity through Versatility. Do not Fear what you do not know and do not be deterred if you do not succeed at first. Build Resiliency by being Defiant with Morality. Be Honorable and Trustworthy as you encounter new people. If you can offer Loyalty, remember that Generosity does not always get reciprocated in ways we expect, so avoid Melancholy if your expectations should be seemingly unmet. Do not Guilt anybody into doing anything they do not want to do and do your best to avoid these traps as well. If you do your best to do all of this on your journey through life, then I would safely say people would be Lucky to have you in their lives. The same is true for the ones we come across that have a positive effect on us, we would be fortunate to encounter such great people and it will always behoove us to find value in every situation, no matter how bleak it may seem. Afterall, our situations are a matter of Perception. If we can be Patient and Considerate of others, we may be viewed as someone who is Reliable, thus Motivating others to follow our lead as we follow those with more Wisdom than ourselves. To some, it is a matter of fulfilling a Duty. The best we can hope for is that in our best moments, we will have Serenity which will allow us to re-align as needed and give us level heads so that we can prepare for whatever else is to come, because there is always something else coming.

The Final Takeaway: We must first be willing to observe and listen to our fellow man before we can have a full appreciation for their Perception. The same is true for those we attempt to guide when applicable. We must realize that participating in life is essential to gaining more complete knowledge and overall experience. Each are critical in earning the right to offering Wisdom in its entirety.

ACKNOWLEDGEMENTS

This is a portion of the piece designated more specifically to those that have been there for me when I was down for the count. My dad has liked and shared the hell out of the social media posts I made trying to self-promote Volume 1, his place for recognition belongs at the top of this list. Practicing what I preach: doing the best we can with what we have, is truly a virtue I got from him in so many ways.

My fellow co-workers that were there for me when I needed it most, you guys made ALL the difference. Your place in my life is greater than you could know, as I am proud to admit crying behind the bar in front of dozens of people, feeling so much love overwhelm me. You guys have a very small idea of the impact you made, but now for everyone to see, you made a tremendous impact. The kids received a Christmas I could not give them. You literally saved me from more hardship, which is priceless in my book, and I cannot thank you enough. Not to mention, all of your Moral support both direct and indirect. I know where your hearts are, and it means the world to me. Thank you all so, so much!

Anyone that followed me on social media and liked or shared my posts, I sincerely appreciate you. Getting Volume 1 out on my own was not as productive as you might think, but it is my place in history that you can all proudly stake your claim as assisting along the way. Every individual that had a genuine interest is appreciated. I held a raffle not long after Volume 1 was published. Miss Franny O. won the raffle and is someone I look up to and admire.

I was fortunate enough to meet people along the way that enjoyed Volume 1 and provided critical feedback that I feel has helped me design Volume 2 in a more productive way. Hopefully this was evident as you trudged through my scenarios and inconspicuous humor. The messages outlined are merely hubs, if you will, or reference points for you to use to form your own opinions and Perception. Anyway, these few people helped add to how I went about writing Volume 2 and I sincerely hope it was in a way that readers can understand and Respect. To the few of you that I spoke to personally and consulted with about concepts and ideas, thank you so much for your time, efforts and input. Whether you see a difference in my writing that you affected or not, I assure you that our conversations were on my mind throughout.

To everyone I have not yet met, I hope to someday. Your support means the world, and your actions affected by what you have absorbed mean even more. You are on your journey, just like everyone else. Do your best to show Respect, Accept life as it comes and earn Wisdom through experience. Above all else, be kind. The world is not yours and it's certainly not mine. We live in it together, so share the damn thing!

THE TAKEAWAYS:

SERENITY: *Finding peace is imperative to maintaining sanity. This seems obvious enough, yet many of us are gluttons for punishment and allow ourselves to get pushed to the limit before we finally snap and push back. We need to do our best to avoid snapping. We need to find a backdrop and go there consistently to achieve Serenity for the sake of our mental health as well as humanity.*

GENEROSITY: You do not have to spend hundreds of dollars or pay for someone's coffee without them knowing. You can simply start by holding the door open for someone. Tell your co-worker when they have a booger hanging out of their nose, or just laugh at a stupid joke after you imagine your co-worker with a booger hanging from their nose. In all seriousness, Generosity takes a lot of character. All I can really ask at this point is that you deliver an act of Generosity where you are comfortable, but never expect one when you're not.

LUCK: It is okay to have superstitions and good Luck charms or rituals. It's also okay to believe that every time you make a certain gesture or wear your Lucky T-shirt that your team is destined to win. However, don't get upset when it doesn't work. Take Luck for what it is; a matter of Perception. The lower your expectations are, the Luckier you will be, unless you're downrange of a Triple 7, then you're kind of screwed. Good Luck with that!

LOYALTY & TRUST: In case you did not hear me before; When you earn Respect, you gain Trust. When you gain Trust, you can begin to build Loyalty. It takes a monumental amount of time to build a reputation, and your Trustworthiness and Loyalties should be apparent in that reputation. Be aware of your true intentions, for that reputation that takes so long to build can be completely destroyed in a matter of seconds.

SELFLESSNESS: Being Selfless is no easy task. It requires us to put our needs second to someone else's. We look past what we want in life and shift Focus off of ourselves. Being letdown is only a possibility if our expectations exceed realistic capabilities within given circumstances. As long as we are

Patient, our Generosity should be recognized at some point and paid forward over time, just as we need to be mindful of someone else's Generosity and Patience. We must remember to stay human and be more human than human for the sake of the future.

DUTY & HONOR: *Duty and Honor often go together. Uniformed personnel especially can attest to this (or argue against it), but the fact of the matter is; It is dishonorable to ignore or even object a sense of Duty. You do not need to risk your life to be Honorable but standing with the intention of being Honorable is a great place to start.*

DEFIANCE & RESILIENCY: *We're all going to get knocked around in life. The sooner we Accept it, the better. The sooner we can identify core issues of Defiance, the sooner we can meet them with our ever-growing Perception, ready to help turn the situation into something productive. No matter how much it hurts, life may kick us while we are down. Remember to get back up and move forward. Every time you do, you build your Resiliency, which is pretty damn awesome.*

MELANCHOLY: *Everyone has down days, and they are absolutely okay. Talk about what is bothering you and deal with issues in a mature, well-communicated manner. This is the best possible way you and others will come to Create a positive, more productive environment together. Look out for yourself as well as others. You just never know when you may save someone's life without realizing it.*

FEAR: *Fear is inevitable and frankly, it is necessary. We need Fear to react to situations naturally. We experience Fear in many different ways as we grow older. The more your Fears shift, the more you are growing or at least shifting Focus in life. You have a Perception that is still blooming, but Fear should always be a part of it. The same two questions will always remain in place that you should be able to answer at any time; "What are you afraid of?, And, How do you respond to Fear? What really matters is how you face Fear. In other words, don't be afraid to be in Fear, just don't let it rule your life.*

CONFIDENCE: *Being Confident takes choosing Confidence before it is earned. The experiences we face are all opportunities in one light or another. Face your Fears to overcome them, but ideally when you are prepared to do so. Do not Fear failure, embrace triumph but be humble in the Confidence you build, before a bigger Confidence tests your Resiliency. Keep on Keeping on.*

ACCEPTANCE: *We all have our views in life. Some of us like the Cowboys, some of us like being cowboys, some care about neither and others dislike the Cowboys but like cowboys. (Confused as I am?) The real point is to Accept circumstances and life for what it is. This is the critical step in life that allows us to properly identify a situation so that we can work towards a higher quality of life not just for ourselves, but everyone involved. Accept these words and you will continue heading down a path or greater Perception.*

CLOSURE: *A major part of gaining Closure is Accepting what has happened. If you are in a situation you need Closure for, pain is inevitable, so brace yourself as best you can. Talk to someone, no matter how much you do not want to talk. It's okay to be down, just don't let life keep you there.*

GUILT: *No one should ever enjoy feeling Guilt, but it is inevitable for us humans. Guilt is the soul's way of saying, "Hey, you probably shouldn't have done that, but you did so I'm going to keep sitting on you until you make it better." Be Respectable and have Integrity. It is okay to make mistakes, so long as we learn from them and acknowledge and make amends with the people that may have been hurt along the way, including ourselves.*

VERSATILITY: *Honestly, Versatility is not for everyone, nor is it entirely necessary. It's up to you if you want to live life like a Swiss Army Knife, being equipped to complete several diverse tasks without depending on someone else to do them for you. If that's not for you, it doesn't have to be. No matter how you run your motor, remember that dealing with negative energy in a positive was is one of the most important ways we can keep ourselves burning clean, positive energy.*

CREATIVITY: *Curiosity is the base of Creativity. If you deny your curiosity to run its course within reason, then you stifle your own Creativity and you subject yourself to becoming another average Joe or Jill, following the rest of the followers as they go through the motions of life. If that's all you want to do, that's fine, but always use your blinkers and stay out of the fast lane when the rest of the world wants to pass you.*

MOTIVATION: *Motivation is a very powerful thing. It is as simple as that. If we can figure out what Motivates us, then we can ideally plan our lives accordingly. We are also highly likely to tie our Motivation to whatever it is we are Passionate about. If you are in a place or can get to a place where your Passion perpetually fuels your Motivation and vice versa, then you are doing a hell of a job at life. Hopefully your Passion contributes to society in a positive* way so as to inspire others that they too can unlock the Motivation-Passion loop. (Officially calling this the Mo-Pa loop.)

WISDOM: *We must first be willing to observe and listen to our fellow man before we can have a full appreciation for their Perception. The same is true for those we attempt to guide when applicable. We must realize that participating in life is essential to gaining more complete knowledge and overall experience. Each are critical in earning the right to offering Wisdom in its entirety.*

REFERENCES

Cuddy, A. (2011, June 2). *Amy Cuddy: Power Poses.* [Video file]. Retrieved from http://www.youtube.com/watch?v=pchDQ0H LnY&feature=share

Dove, L. (2015, June 17). "Why is a rabbit's foot considered lucky?". Retrieved from http://people.howstuffworks.com/rabbt-foot-luck. htm>9December2019

Kime, P. (2019, August 1). Military Suicides Reach Highest Rate Since Record-Keeping Began After 9/11. Retrieved from https://www. military.com/daily-news/2019/08/01/pentagon-reports-record-number-suicides.html

Lee, K. (2019). Effective Ways to Handle Defiant Children. Retrieved from https://www.verywellfamily.com/how-to-handle-defiant-children-620106

Raga, S. (2016). 14 Good Luck Superstitions from Around the World. Retrieved from http://www.mentalfloss.com/article/79409/14-good-luck-superstitions-around-world

Rogers, M. (2019). Doctors Tell Us How Hiking Can Change Our Brains. Retrieved from http://www.lifehack.org/363786/doctors-agree--hiking-good-for-your-mental-health.

ABOUT THE AUTHOR

Like you, I have dreams. I have been doing my best to work through the Covid-19 pandemic, just like everybody else. Life has certainly changed in a big way since this whole thing started, and I believe life will never return to the way we knew it. That being said, you should know that I too have changed since Hindsight Volume 1.

I went from bartending in a casino to being unemployed for a while. I made an attempt to trade stocks on the side but did not generate enough capital to sustain daily life. I have saved pop cans, cleaned houses, picked up odd jobs and even went to work for an Amazon delivery fleet just to make ends meet.

I have considered going back into the military and going back to school. I have thought about starting my own business based around the things I do to get by, but none of those things hold my attention or passion like writing does.

I will continue to write, with enhanced perspective based around not only my experiences, but of those around me. I draw from my memories, experiences, and observations to develop something I hope you can relate to one way or another. I hope my words find relevance because if I did not feel they needed to be said, I would not say them to begin with.

We breathe the same air and we drink the same water. We see the same moon and live by the grace of the same sun. We are all human (until you can prove otherwise), and I am here to contribute something meaningful and unique to our very short time on this earth. Again, I hope these words find you well, no matter where you are in life.

Printed in the United States
By Bookmasters